TARANTULAS

Andreas Tinter
Translator: William Charlton
Photos by the author unless otherwise credited.

yearBOOK

Until a few years ago it was nearly impossible to buy general literature on tarantulas. Recently, however, a number of authors, several of whom I may count among my circle of friends, have published tarantula books. This book is written mainly for the beginner, but for advanced hobbyists as well, who will surely be able to find useful information even if they have kept tarantulas for a fairly long time. At this time I would like to thank all those who offered me assistance. My special thanks go to my friend Michael Bullmer, who made a substantial contribution to the success of most of the photography. My thanks also go to Mrs. Susanne Leidenroth from the Stattlichen Museum fur Naturkunde (State Museum of Natural History) in Stuttgart, who prepared many contrast electron micrographs of the bulbs of male tarantulas.

Andreas Tinter
Kornwestheim, Germany

What are YearBOOKs?

Because keeping Tarantulas as pets is growing at a rapid pace, information on their selection, care and breeding is vitally needed in the marketplace. Books, the usual way information of this sort is transmitted, can be too slow. Sometimes by the time a book is written and published, the material contained therein is a year or two old...and no new material has been added during that time. Only a book in a magazine form can bring breaking stories and current information. A magazine is streamlined in production, so we have adopted certain magazine publishing techniques in the creation of this yearBOOK. Magazines also can be much cheaper than books because they are supported by advertising. To combine these assets into a great publication, we issued this yearBOOK in both magazine and book format at different prices.

yearBOOKS,INC.
Dr. Herbert R. Axelrod,
Founder & Chairman
Neal Pronek
Chief Editor
Jerry G. Walls
Editor

yearBOOKS are all photo composed, color separated and designed on Scitex equipment in Neptune, N.J. with the following staff:

DIGITAL PRE-PRESS
Michael L. Secord
Supervisor
Robert Onyrscuk
Jose Reyes
Computer Art
Sherise Buhagiar
Patti Escabi
Cynthia Fleureton
Sandra Taylor Gale
Pat Marotta
Joanne Muzyka

Advertising Sales
George Campbell
Chief
Amy Manning
Director
Jennifer Feidt
Coordinator

Originally published in German by bede-Verlag under the title *Erfolg mit Vogelspinnen*. Copyright by bede-Verlag.

©yearBOOKS,Inc.
1 TFH Plaza
Neptune, N.J. 07753
Completely manufactured in Neptune, N.J.
USA

CONTENTS

INDEX
OF TECHNICAL TERMS

abdomen: hindmost body division
adult: fully grown
bulb: male reproductive organ
carapace: covering of the cephalothorax
cephalothorax: foremost body division
chelicerae: biting fangs with basal segment
coxa: first leg segment from the body out
exuvia: molted skin
femur: third leg segment from the body out
labium: lower lip
metatarsus: sixth leg segment from the body out
opisthosoma: abdomen
patella: fourth leg segment from the body out
pedipalp: feeler
prosoma: cephalothorax
spermatheca: female sperm sac
tarsus: seventh leg segment from the body out
tibia: fifth leg segment from the body out
trochanter: second leg segment from the body out

A female *Grammostola spatulata.*

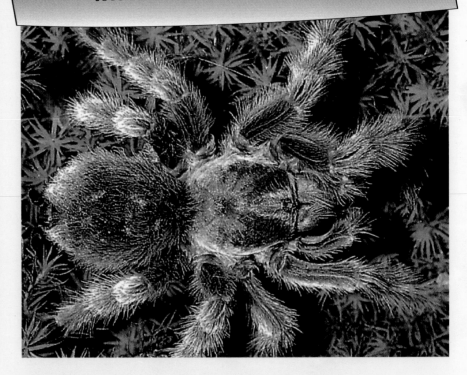

INTRODUCTION

The terrarium hobby has become increasingly popular in recent years. After decades of domination by the aquarium hobby, more and more animal lovers are deciding in favor of a terrarium. Within the general terrarium hobby, however, the keeping of tarantulas holds a special position, because the keeping requirements of tarantulas differ greatly from those of reptiles or amphibians. In the meantime, the accessory market has reacted to this development and for some time has even offered specialized terraria and specialized accessories for keeping tarantulas. This simplifies entry into the hobby, particularly for the beginner, who up to a few years ago was left to his or her own resources. Very few pet shops carried tarantulas, and dealers seldom knew anything about proper care. This situation has improved substantially, so today even the beginner can take great pleasure in his charges from the start.

In general, tarantulas are relatively easy to keep and do not require enormous expense. Nonetheless, we must consider a few points. With this book I will try not only to provide an introduction and good tips to the beginner that I have accumulated from my own many years of experience, but also to give a few new suggestions to those who already keep tarantulas. Over the last years I have occupied myself very intensively with the various topics associated with the theraphosids (tarantulas), and am also well traveled in this matter. I would like to pass on all these experiences.

Certainly there is room for discussion of some points, particularly as far as keeping and several other topics are concerned. There certainly are slight differences in keeping practices, and each person will keep his or her tarantulas somewhat differently. In my book, however, I will primarily draw on my own experiences and the techniques with which I have had good success so far and which also will prove very valuable to the reader.

I therefore wish you much enjoyment in the reading of this book and in the care of your charges.

Fundamental considerations

We should give careful consideration to the acquisition of any animal. Although a tarantula is not nearly as time-consuming to care for as most other pets, we can encounter problems under certain circumstances that we should consider beforehand. I would like to address several of these problems here, because this could spare a hobbyist from unnecessary annoyance and cost. The experiences I was able to accumulate on my second job in a pet shop are a big help here. While there, I noticed that people repeatedly bought animals without having considered the ramifications of owning a pet. It often turned out that they found it impossible to keep the pet for some reason or other, or the animal became sick or even died through the lack of relevant information. For this reason I advise you to gather as much information as possible before you acquire a pet.

Acanthoscurria antillensis, female.

Before the purchase, you should consider the following points:

Do I have enough time for the animal?

The time needed to care for a tarantula is relatively small in comparison to other pets. Nonetheless, you should have a few spare hours a week that you can split up over the individual days. A properly furnished terrarium does not necessarily require daily care, and if you take a few precautions you even can safely go on vacation without having to worry about your charges. You will, however, have to devote some time to care for the tarantulas.

Do your family members and housemates approve?

Not infrequently this hobby meets with misunderstanding or even repugnance, and many a tenant is allergic to his or her new subtenant. I am familiar with one case in which an acquaintance of mine was given an ultimatum by his wife: the spiders or me. Although he thought long and hard, he eventually decided in favor of his wife.

Can I deal with the food animals?

Naturally, tarantulas also need something to eat. The diet consists primarily of insects, as well as mice with the larger species. Therefore, whoever cannot hold or at least handle crickets, grasshoppers, cockroaches, and possibly mice should reconsider acquiring a tarantula.

Am I allergic?

Some tarantula species have irritating hairs on the opisthosoma (abdomen) that they either brush off when threatened or use to line their dens to discourage undesirable guests. Each person reacts differently to these irritating hairs. Some people do not react at all, while others can develop facial swelling or suffer from sneezing and watery eyes. We cannot predict how each individual will react. The only way to tell is to come into contact with the tarantulas. Additionally, many tarantula species do not have irritating hairs. If you have doubts, you must test your physical reaction to the particular tarantula.

What are my feelings toward tarantulas?

Certainly no one who has an absolute aversion to tarantulas will buy one of these animals. It is just as important, however, not to become totally infatuated with them. I, at least, received my first spider with mixed feelings. On the one hand, I was somewhat fearful and at least cautious because of the widespread fairy tales about how dangerous and poisonous tarantulas are, but, on the other hand, I was so fascinated by these animals that I absolutely had to learn more about them. Is there a better way to do this than to keep them in your home? What I mean to say by this is that although, under certain circumstances, a little courage is necessary at the start to acquire a tarantula, you should not be afraid, because basically nothing can happen. In the following chapter I will give tips on which spiders are more suitable for the beginner and which are not.

Finally, *I ask that no one acquire a tarantula from a craving for the sensational,* because the animal will certainly suffer and often will come to harm through frequent handling and showing. Unfortunately, we repeatedly find such people. Unfortunately, I also realize that my appeal will not dissuade them.

Which species should I acquire?

Once you have decided to acquire a tarantula, the next thing you should do is to decide what species it should be. The type of terrarium and furnishings depend on this choice.

We fundamentally divide tarantulas into terrestrial and arboreal species. Terrestrial species live in the wild primarily in more or less deep dens in the ground or under rocks. They rarely climb trees or bushes and usually leave their dens only at night. Of the minimum of 850 tarantula species known to science, the majority are terrestrial. They include peaceful and aggressive species. In contrast to their arboreal relatives, terrestrial tarantulas need a low terrarium with a larger floor space. At this point I can recommend only a few genera that normally have a peaceful temperament. Among these I include, in any case, most of the species of the genera *Brachypelma* and *Grammostola,* which are often offered in the pet trade. A few species of the genus *Pamphobeteus* are also quite peaceful and still reach an impressive size. It is best simply to test the animal before the purchase to see if it is aggressive. You do this by teasing the animal a little with a small rod. If the tarantula

A female *Avicularia versicolor*. These metallic tree-dwelling tarantulas have become very popular pets.

does not raise its front legs or strike at the rod, it is not unduly aggressive. Among the terrestrial species, virtually all Asian and African species are aggressive and are not particularly suitable for the beginner. With the arboreal species, the aggressiveness in relation to the provenance is the same as with the terrestrial forms. Here too, the species from Asia and Africa tend to be aggressive. On the other hand, some of these aggressive species are quite attractive. With the New World tarantulas, most species are quite peaceful. The perfect example here is the genus *Avicularia*, which includes many species that we can describe as being peaceful. This genus is therefore well represented on the market and is popular with and coveted by many

hobbyists. This genus also includes quite colorful species. These species need a taller terrarium with a smaller floor space because they build the silk nests in which they live high above the ground. Most arboreal tarantulas unfortunately have an unpleasant habit: they spray their excrement in a high arc from the silk nest. The excrement then usually lands on the terrarium glass, which has driven many a hobbyist to despair, particularly if they like to keep a clean terrarium.

Which tarantula you ultimately acquire is your own choice. I advise all beginners, however, to start with a peaceful species to gain experience. Later we can also keep the more aggressive species. I will discuss how to handle them in a later chapter.

In any case, first set up your terrarium, furnish it, and operate it for several days without a tarantula, to make sure that you have achieved the required conditions in the terrarium. Otherwise it could happen that you will be put under pressure and your tarantula could suffer from it.

I recommend, if possible, buying captive-bred specimens, because they tend to be healthier and hardier than wild-caught tarantulas. Furthermore, in this way we do not take anything from the wild. Some pet shops already sell only captive-bred tarantulas.

You should also make sure, if you want to buy a protected *Brachypelma smithi*, to obtain a CITES certificate from the buyer, because this, and at the moment only this, species is listed in Appendix II of CITES.

THE TERRARIUM

Choosing the terrarium and furnishings

The question of which type of terrarium is appropriate for which spider is relatively easy to answer. Terrestrial spiders need a terrarium with a large floor space in proportion to its height. In this type of terrarium the height should not exceed 40 centimeters (16 inches), because it is possible that the spider, even if it is fundamentally terrestrial, could climb the terrarium glass and take a fall. If it lands on its abdomen on a hard object, it could burst, which usually leads to the spider's death. The size and area of the terrarium depend on the size of the spider. For large species, such as *Pamphobeteus* species, we should offer an area of 30 x 40 centimeters (12 x 16 inches). For medium-sized species, an area of 30 x 30 centimeters (12 x 12 inches) is sufficient, and for small species, such as the dwarf tarantulas of the subfamily Ischnocolinae, a terrarium of 30 x 20 centimeters (12 x 8 inches) is adequate. Naturally, we can also use a larger terrarium, but it will not increase the spider's well-being. Rather, we can use it for decorative reasons, because we can furnish a larger terrarium more attractively. The only disadvantage of very large terraria is that the food animals can hide more easily in them, which can cause

problems, for example, in the molt. We will return to this subject later.

The terraria available on the market are offered in the most diverse sizes and variations. Many of them, however, are unsuitable. Nonetheless, there are two types that I would like to emphasize, because they offer different benefits. The difference lies primarily in how we close them. On the one hand, there are terraria with a vertical sliding door that can be pulled out when pushed completely upward. These terraria are highly

escape-proof without special precautions, because the sliding glass is automatically pulled downward by gravity. I have yet to see a spider that could escape from such a terrarium.

The second variant has two horizontal sliding panes that slide along a double-U track and can be pressed against each other. Here the tarantula has the opportunity, if it is strong enough, to open a crack between the two panes and escape. Therefore, we should lock this terrarium with an appropriately bent

It is sensible to use a screen cover on your tank when housing your tarantula. Some are equipped with locking devices that will prevent your tarantula from getting out. Photo courtesy of Four Paws.

A variety of light bulbs suitable for use in the terrarium can be found at your local pet shop. Photo courtesy of Energy Savers.

paper clip. This system, however, does have an advantage. There are special locks available on the market that we can use to lock the terrarium securely. This has the additional advantage of preventing unauthorized people from opening the terrarium. This is quite practical, particularly in families with children.

Either type of terrarium should have ventilation openings. If they are arranged diagonally the terrarium glass normally will not fog up.

For the well being of tarantulas, we should maintain a temperature of 22 to 25°C (72 to 77°F) in the terrarium. Because this is above normal room temperature, we usually need some help. We can reach the required temperature with an incandescent bulb of appropriate wattage that we install in the terrarium or with a heating pad that we install on the outside glass of the terrarium. We should never place the heating pad under the terrarium, because it will warm the substrate, which is an unnatural condition for a tarantula. If a tarantula digs a burrow in the wild, with increasing depth it always becomes moister and cooler. If it digs in a terrarium that is heated from below, the substrate becomes increasingly warmer and drier. If it stays in this burrow, it can come to harm or even die.

We also need other utensils for control and feeding. Every terrarium, for example,

should have a thermometer and if possible a hygrometer so that we can easily and constantly monitor the temperature and humidity. We also need a water dish, which should be as heavy as possible (clay or ceramic), because tarantulas occasionally redecorate their terrarium to their own satisfaction and could tip over a water dish if it were too light. We also need long stainless steel forceps to put the food insects where we want them in the terrarium without losing them. Many of my tarantulas now take the food directly from the forceps, without my having to drop the food insect in the terrarium.

When we have these things in place, we can move on to the furnishing of the terrarium.

Furnishing and setting up the terrarium

There are a number of different ways to furnish a tarantula terrarium. I would categorize the various methods as ranging from Spartan to decorative. In any case, we need a substrate. For this purpose I use simple potting soil, which may contain fertilizer but must not be treated with insecticides. We also can use pure peat, but it has the disadvantage that if we allow it to dry out it is very difficult to moisten again. The substrate should be at least 6 to 8 centimeters (2.5 to 3 inches) deep. The deeper the substrate, the better it holds moisture.

Roots of all kinds, cork bark, and rocks are suitable for furnishing the terrarium. To minimize the danger of injury from falls, we should not position them too close to

A furnished terrarium for arboreal species. Make sure that the terrarium is not exposed to direct sunlight, because it could overheat.

species rearrange their terrarium after a certain amount of time and then literally leave no stone upon another.

Always make sure that you do not set up your terrarium by a window or in a place the sun can shine directly on it. When exposed to direct sunlight in this way, it will heat up strongly in a short time. If the temperature rises above 30°C (86°F), the tarantula will die quickly.

Keeping conditions

Unlike other terrarium animals, tarantulas are quite easy to keep, and they thrive as long as we consider a few basic requirements. We do not necessarily need to look in on them every day, although this, of course, would be beneficial.

For the majority of tarantulas, a temperature of 22 to 25°C (72 to 77°F) and a humidity of 70 to 80 percent are the correct values. A few species are an exception, because they, for example, come from higher altitudes with lower prevailing temperatures. Such species were considered to be difficult to keep until it was discovered that they simply needed a cooler climate. When wholesalers import animals, they usually provide no information on the provenance of the spiders. Thus, we often know nothing about the keeping conditions of new species. Accordingly, we have no choice but to keep the tarantulas under normal or "average" conditions and hope that they correspond to the natural living conditions.

One species that was considered to be problematic was *Megaphobema*

the side glass. A fairly large piece of curved cork bark, if we place it on the substrate, can serve a terrestrial species as a hiding place or even a den. If we position it vertically, it can provide an arboreal species a place to attach its silk nest. I furnish my terraria with these objects. If you want to make the terrarium somewhat more attractive, you can add plants. You should buy plants, however, that are

hardy and do not need too much light, such as ivy, ornamental vines, or mosses. In any case we must wash the plants thoroughly to remove any insecticides that may be present. A planting is certainly very attractive, but it usually means considerable expense, because the plants usually survive only for a short time. You can only hope that your tarantula will "like" the furnishings, because certain

mesomelas, which has been imported at irregular intervals for a few years. At first we did not know that the species came from the mountainous region around Monteverde in Costa Rica, which tends to be covered with fog and has a rather cool climate. They live in shallow dens excavated in the damp soil. There is a prevailing fresh wind there as well. We were not aware of these conditions until hobbyists traveled to Costa Rica and studied the climate. Subsequently we kept the species under cooler and moister conditions in the terrarium, which resulted in a sharp increase in the survival rate. The fact that this species was bred extremely rarely indicates that the keeping conditions were not optimal and that the tarantulas had to adapt to the microclimate in the terrarium over a fairly long time. Another species that we should keep under cooler conditions in the terrarium is *Hapalotremus albipes* from Bolivia. When this species was first imported it also presented keeping problems.

We achieve the desired temperature of 22 to 25°C (72 to 77°F) by using an incandescent bulb or a heating pad. All we need to do is to determine the wattage of the light bulb necessary to achieve the desired temperature. With the terrarium sizes mentioned previously, approximately 25 watts are necessary. The situation is a little more complicated with a heating pad or heating cable, because we have to choose a wattage at the time of purchase. It should have an output of at

least 50 watts, because the efficiency is reduced when we install it outside the terrarium. If the terrarium becomes too warm with the heating pad in constant use, we should switch the pad on and off at regular intervals with a timer. In this way we reduce the temperature inside the terrarium. We will have to use trial and error here until we discover the right setting. Furthermore, the accessory market offers complete control units that use a thermocouple inside the terrarium and a thermostat to maintain the desired temperature. It is even possible to set the unit to lower the temperature at night.

We achieve the correct humidity in the terrarium by spraying, watering the substrate, or a combination of the two. With arboreal species, spraying is indispensable because they usually drink from the drops of water on the furnishings. We should not spray the spider itself directly, because it will not like it and usually will run away. The reason for this is that certain hairs of tarantulas are sense organs that react to the slightest fluctuations in the air. If we spray the spider, it is the same as boxing its ears. With my terrestrial species I only water the substrate, because this usually is sufficient for maintaining the correct humidity. Moreover, if we spray with hard tap water, we usually end up with many calcium spots on the glass that are hard to remove.

Before going on vacation, we should wet the substrate very well. The day we leave we should put the terrarium in a cool room (about 18°C, 65°F)

and turn off the heat. This ensures that the humidity will be maintained for a fairly long time. A lower temperature over several weeks usually will not harm the spider. Sometimes a temporary change in climate can even bring the tarantulas into breeding condition or stimulate the female to build a cocoon.

It goes without saying that the water dish, which must be present in the bottom of the terrarium, must always be kept clean and filled. Unfortunately, some specimens have the habit of excreting their droppings into the water dish, which means, of course, that we must change the drinking water daily.

Routine maintenance

The daily maintenance tasks include spraying or moistening the substrate and cleaning and filling the water dish. Furthermore, several times a week we must check for food remains or dead food animals in the terrarium, which we must remove to eliminate a possible source of infection. Excrement on the substrate is almost impossible to find, and as long as fungus does not grow, we can ignore it. Even excrement on the glass is only a nuisance, because it dries hard and does no harm. Therefore, the routine daily maintenance amounts to only 5 to 10 minutes per terrarium.

If the terrarium is very soiled, we should empty it and clean it and the furnishings thoroughly. At this time we also can replenish the plantings if we wish.

HANDLING TARANTULAS

Handling tarantulas is a headache, particularly to the beginner, because he or she has no idea how the spiders will react to being touched. Each individual, in fact, reacts differently. We can safely say from the start, however, that we do not have to pick up a tarantula by hand. Moreover, handling tarantulas is far less dangerous than we might assume. In the many years that I have kept tarantulas I have not been bitten a single time. One reason for this is that I have exercised a certain amount of caution from the start. The other reason is that I have always accepted the spider as a "wild" animal and have treated it accordingly. Naturally, once in a while, such as for demonstration purposes for school children, I do pick up a tarantula with my fingers and let it walk over my hands and those of the enthusiastic children. This is not possible, however, with every specimen.

Many species are aggressive by nature and can only be picked up after a great deal of practice. We need not necessarily do this with our fingers either, because another aid is available. The cheapest and most dependable aid is the plastic container that we have left over from our first purchase of food insects. We can, however, also use any other kind of plastic container. It is beneficial, however, if it is transparent.

When we must remove the tarantula from the terrarium, such as for cleaning, we simply put an empty

If you are looking for substrate that is easy to work with and also is easy to clean, a terrarium liner will do nicely. Photo courtesy of Four Paws.

container over the spider. Then we push the lid under the container and close it. In this way our spider is stored safely and we can get on with our work. Depending on the tarantula species, we must move more or less quickly. Should the spider happen to threaten us during this procedure, we do not have to worry. The plastic container is a good protective shield through which the spider is unable to bite.

Another method is to grasp the spider with large, long stainless steel forceps. These forceps should be at least 30 centimeters (12 inches) long. To grasp the tarantula, hold the forceps horizontally and approach the spider from the side. Finally, grip it by the cephalothorax at the point between the second and

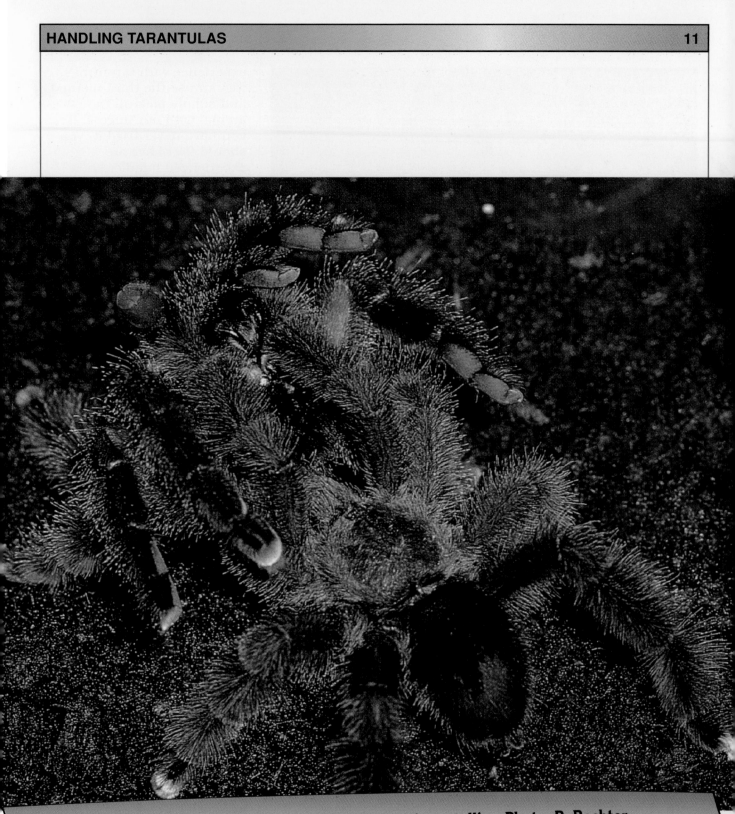

A mating pair of the spectacular arboreal *Avicularia metallica*. Photo: R. Bechter.

Here we see an example of how to pick up a tarantula with the aid of long forceps. Grip the spider from the side by the cephalothorax between the second and third pairs of legs. You must never squeeze too hard, as you need to avoid injuring the spider. The pressure must be strong enough, however, that the spider cannot escape.

third pairs of legs. Make sure that you do not squeeze too tightly, but tightly enough that the spider cannot get away. Do not worry, because the spider's body is quite solid in this place and with a little care on your part the

tarantula will suffer no harm. When we grasp and lift the spider in this way, it usually spreads its legs and we can turn and rotate it, which can be an advantage for determining the sex.

If we already have some

experience with tarantulas, we can use the third method and simply pick up the animal with our fingers. If you have never tried it, you should first have an experienced handler show you how to do it and then practice with a peaceful specimen.

With this method you press the spider's cephalothorax to the ground with your index finger so that it cannot run away and cannot defend itself. Then, with the thumb and middle finger of the same hand, you take a firm grip on the cephalothorax between the second and third pairs of legs. If the spider tries to free itself, you must either squeeze harder or put the specimen down again and apply a new grip. This method takes some practice, and we should use it only with specimens that are not aggressive.

How we should handle a particular spider is a matter of experience. We cannot pick up *Pamphobeteus nigricolor* from Ecuador, for example, with forceps, let alone with our fingers. Once gripped the spider tries to free itself persistently, which this large and strong spider will eventually manage to do. Here we must use the plastic-container method, which also is the safest technique.

If we must handle an aggressive tarantula, because, for example, the spider is injured or has molted poorly, we capture the specimen with a plastic container and put it in the refrigerator for several minutes. The low temperature will reduce greatly the spider's physical activity, which gives us the opportunity, if the spider has not warmed up again, to perform the necessary task. In a number of research institutes a special apparatus is used to immobilize spiders so they can be examined. Here the spider is exposed to carbon dioxide for up to a half hour, which renders it completely motionless. This method is quite expensive, however, and should only be used by experienced people.

If we must send a tarantula by mail, there are certain things we must take into account. It is basically permitted to send invertebrate animals in the normal mail, though often there might be specific prohibitions against mailing tarantulas and you might have to use a private delivery service. We should, however, always send spiders by the fastest delivery possible. The most important factor here is how we pack the spider. Because we must assume that the package will be dropped or bumped at some point, it is important that we pack the animal in such a way that it will not be injured by a hard blow. We do this by packing small spiders in empty film containers (the round plastic canisters) in which we have punched holes. Before we put the spider in the film container, we should line it with a piece of paper towel. We then pack the film container itself in shredded newspaper or cotton wool. These materials will insulate the spiders from jolts and

How to pick up a tarantula with the hand. If you have any doubts about your ability to pick up a spider without dropping it, don't try. Even short falls may hurt a tarantula.

blows. We pack spiders that are too big to fit in film containers in small plastic bags. This sounds cruel at first but has proved effective over many years and does not harm the spiders at all. It is best to use plastic bags that are strong (not flimsy) without being brittle. The spider will either walk into the bag itself or we can pick it up with forceps and put it in the bag. Then we drive the spider into a corner of the bag and prevent it from retreating by twisting the bag. Finally we knot the end of the bag so the spider has very little room to move. The spider often bites through the bag. If the material is strong, however, they will not be able to tear it to pieces even if they can bite holes in it. If we humans were put in a plastic bag, we would suffocate in a few minutes. It is different with spiders. Even spending several days in a plastic bag does them no harm. I have had tarantulas that spent almost two weeks in this type of package because they were sent to the wrong address, but they still arrived in good condition.

It is far more dangerous for the spiders if it is very hot or very cold. We absolutely must protect tarantulas from these weather conditions during shipment. On very hot days we should not ship them or at least should equip the package with many ventilation holes. In the winter we probably will have no choice but to use Styrofoam boxes. These provide fairly good insulation and, if necessary, we can heat them with "heat packs," which are paper bags filled with special granules that are vacuum-packed for storage. To use them we remove the bag from the vacuum packaging and, for example, tape it to the cover of the Styrofoam box. The granules in the bag generate heat when they come in contact with oxygen. In the process no noxious gases are released. We must make sure, however, that we do not place the bag in the immediate vicinity of the spiders, because

Citharischius crawshayi. Females have powerful hind legs that they use primarily to excavate deep burrows.

temperatures of up to 50°C (122°F) can develop temporarily. We can buy "heat packs" on the specialist market or from mail-order companies. Recently small reusable packs that can be microwaved have become available; they only hold heat for a day or so, but this may be sufficient for some uses.

THE FOOD

Like all living creatures, tarantulas need food to drive their metabolism. Because of their minimal physical activity, however, they can turn into real starvation artists. I have experienced cases in which, for example, species of the genus *Grammostola* refused to eat for a year or more and still remained healthy. This is not the rule, of course, but can occur in exceptional cases. Therefore, do not be disturbed if one of your charges fasts for a long time.

However, there is the other extreme. *Theraphosa leblondi*, for example, has a strong tendency to overeat, which can stretch the abdomen to gigantic proportions. Klaas, a colleague of mine, once reported to me in this connection that a female of this species, after devouring a number of mice, had an abdomen the size of a tennis ball. This may seem impressive but usually would not happen in the wild because the food supply there tends to be far more meager. Furthermore, specimens fed in this way are more susceptible to injury because the skin of the abdomen is taut and

could burst because of a slight bump or fall.

The diet of tarantulas can be very varied. We can offer them grasshoppers, crickets, cockroaches, mealworms, giant mealworms, and flies, as well as mice, baby rats, chicks, and small reptiles. We must make sure that the food is not too large or too small. For a spider with a legspan approximately the

Theraphosa leblondi feeding in a burrow. When feeding, as is true of other spiders, try not to disturb the spider any more than necessary.

size of a silver dollar, for example, we should offer a cricket about 1 centimeter (0.5 inch) long. Some species with the same legspan also take larger food animals, while others will scamper away from food of this size. In this case we should give it another try later with smaller food animals. Basically, spiders, unlike

reptiles, do not need a varied food supply. Therefore, the diet can consist of whatever is available. The large species, such as *Theraphosa leblondi*, species of the genera *Pamphobeteus, Xenesthis, Sericopelma,* and others, can be readily and effectively satiated with mice. With a little luck the spiders also will take dead mice. This has the advantage that

we can freeze the mice and then thaw them as needed. The same applies to chicks and baby rats. Before feeding, we do not have to treat the food with vitamins or calcium, as with reptiles.

Not all spiders eat everything that we offer them. It can happen that some species, for example, refuse certain cockroach species. In such cases the spiders then drop the food animal after a short time. We should make sure that we only offer as many food animals as the spider can eat by the end of the following day. Should the spider refuse the offered food, we should remove it from the terrarium. It is possible that the spider is ready to molt. If crickets are in the terrarium during the molting process, it can happen that these food animals will eat the spider. During the molt the tarantula cannot defend itself. An injury can lead to bleeding and death. Furthermore, a tarantula hunting an adult mouse is exposed to another danger. Although it has never happened with my spiders, I have been told that mice have defended themselves after the spider has bitten them and have in turn bitten the spider. This can lead to serious injury or the loss of a leg. My experiences have shown, however, that the tarantula, before it bites, usually quickly feels the mouse with its pedipalps to determine where the mouse's head is. After that, it usually bites the mouse on the nape. The spider's venom does not work particularly fast with warm-blooded animals, so the fight to the death can last a minute or more if the mouse does not die immediately from a broken neck.

The spider often wraps the captured food animal in silk before feeding, or it spins a small web on the ground upon which it devours the victim. The significance of the web has not been researched thoroughly, but it is assumed that in this way even the smallest parts of the prey, such as the legs of insects, will not be lost and can be devoured. In the wild, with a meager food supply, this can be very important.

The spider digests the food outside the mouth opening; that is, the tarantula injects enzymes into the prey animal. The enzymes predigest and liquefy the food, after which the spider sucks it out. This process can produce unpleasant odors, particularly with warm-blooded animals. After the meal, often only indigestible fragments remain, which in insects consist of the chitinous parts, wings, and so forth, and in mice of the fur and tail. To devour a cricket, a medium-sized spider needs about an hour; for a fully grown mouse, often more than 24 hours.

Most spiders live off stored reserves; that is, the keeper does not always have to have food in the house. As a rule, a feeding every one to two weeks is sufficient. If you feed your spider daily, it can happen after a few days that the animal will refuse the food because it has had its fill.

We can determine the state of nutrition of spiders by the circumference of the abdomen. Spiders with a small abdomen are poorly fed, while those with a large abdomen are well fed. This, however, is not true of adult males. After the last molt when they reach maturity, they eat little or nothing at all yet they can retain their mobility and not become sluggish.

You usually can buy food animals in good pet shops.

A male *Poecilotheria regalis.*

Spiders are not insects. Spiders belong to the phylum Arthropoda, which is made up of invertebrates with jointed bodies and limbs. The spiders belong to the subphylum Chelicerata, which are invertebrates lacking antennae. The class Arachnida includes the scorpions, pseudoscorpions, wind-scorpions, daddy-longlegs, mites, and ticks. The tarantulas are classified in the suborder Orthognatha, which also includes the trapdoor spiders and purse-web spiders.

Tarantula systematics

Unfortunately, tarantula systematics has become a tiresome subject. At the moment there are very few people in the world who are seriously working on the systematics of tarantulas. These giant spiders were first mentioned in 1646 by Marcgrave. The first species were formally described by Clerck in 1767. After that, until the end of the nineteenth century, many naturalists worked on the description and classification of spiders, including tarantulas. We are interested specifically in the subfamilies, genera, and species. The following subfamilies of Theraphosidae are relevant today: Harpactirinae, Ornithoctonineae, Thrigmopoeinae, Selenocosmineae, Poecilotherieae, Eumenophorinae, Stromatopelminae,

Aviculariinae, Theraphosinae, Selenogyrinae, and Ischnocolinae. Within these subfamilies we find various genera. As an example I will choose the subfamily Aviculariinae. It contains the following genera: *Avicularia, Psalmopoeus, Pachistopelma, Ephebopus,* and *Tapinauchenius.* Within these genera are the individual species. The genus *Psalmopoeus* contains the species *P. affinis, P. cambridgei, P. ecclesiasitcus, P. intermedius, P. plantaris, P. pulcher, P. reduncus,* and *P. rufus.* If we include all the subfamilies and their genera, at the moment there are approximately 850 different tarantula species.

The scientific names of tarantulas, however, unfortunately sometimes change on the basis of new scientific findings. This is confusing to hobbyists. For example, scientists could determine on the basis of various characters that a species that they had previously classified in genus A, now no longer belongs in this genus. They could put this species in the present genus B or in the new genus C. We cannot rule out, however, that in a few years, on the basis of additional scientific findings, the same species will end up in genus A again. I must admit that this can be very confusing to the layperson.

One of the main reasons for this development is that until now fundamental research has

been lacking. No one is in the position today to name the identifying characters of tarantulas that are 100 percent consistent. Even today we depend on describing in detail all the possible characters and attempt an identification on this basis. No doubt one day someone will make the effort to study hundreds of specimens of the same species for regularities in the characters. After that, a number of identifying characters will surely be derived from the analytical keys.

For this reason I do not wish to present any further systematic classification in this book, but to limit myself to the discussion of the structures.

Important aids for interested readers are the catalogs that have been published since 1942. These catalogs contain the names of all the spiders that were described at the time of their publication, and list the authors of the works and where and when they appeared. The authors of the individual catalogs are Roewer, Bonnet, Brignoli, and Platnick. You can either borrow these catalogs from large libraries or buy them, though some are very expensive. With the help of these catalogs we can find the reference in the literature, which we can use to order the original work or the first description.

Scientific names and identifying tarantulas

The scientific names are certainly the biggest problem,

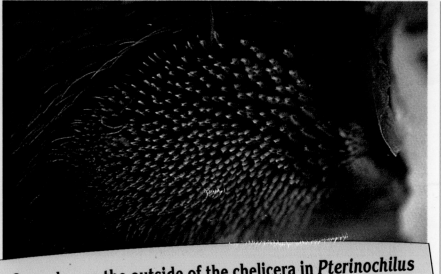

Scopulae on the outside of the chelicera in *Pterinochilus murinus*. The chelicerae are the fangs of tarantulas.

and the beginner, in particular, has a rather hard time with them. The problem is not only that we usually do not know their meaning, but that they are not that easy to pronounce either. I advise my readers not to give up right away, however, because virtually no common names are used with tarantulas, and when they are they regularly lead to misunderstandings. Therefore, it is unavoidable to learn the scientific names of the individual genera and species if you want to join in the conversation.

With the identification of tarantulas I touch upon another, explosive topic, that — and here all noteworthy scientists agree — the majority of tarantulas cannot be distinguished by their coloration or form alone. This is certainly not true of *Brachypelma smithi*, *Brachypelma emilia*, and *Poecilotheria regalis*, to name only a few. There are hundreds of species, however, that are simply brown or black in color,

and here is where the science begins. I bring up this topic because at meetings I am asked repeatedly to identify a particular spider on the spot. I must emphasize time and again that in most cases we need at least one exuvia (skin) of an adult female and a dead adult male preserved in alcohol to identify even the subfamily and genus. Furthermore, information on the locality where the spider was found is of great importance; you should at least know which continent the specimen comes from. If all these things are present, we need a stereomicroscope, stacks of literature, and a few hours to get to the bottom of things. Often we must take various paths to reach our goal; that is, it can happen that we must use several analytical keys to be successful. Even then, as a rule, we can only make a statement about the genus and can then put up for discussion the locality of possible species that come into question. To determine the species exactly,

at least the original description, better yet a direct comparison with the type material, is necessary. So, at your next meeting, if you meet someone who claims to be able to identify tarantulas at a glance, take this with a grain of salt.

THE ANATOMY OF TARANTULAS

Tarantulas, and the remaining members of the suborder Orthognatha, differ from the spiders of the other suborder of spiders, Labidognatha, fundamentally through the position of their chelicerae (biting fangs). In labidognathous spiders the chelicerae move laterally or in and out, whereas in the orthognathous spiders, which include the tarantulas, the chelicerae move vertically or forward and backward. Approximately 90 percent of all spiders belong to the suborder Labidognatha. They include, among others, the crab spiders, comb-footed spiders (including the black widow), wolf spiders, and jumping spiders, to name only a few.

The body of the tarantula is divided fundamentally into the following basic components: the **prosoma (cephalothorax)**, consisting of the carapace (hard dorsal covering), sternum (ventral sclerite), chelicerae, fangs, pedipalps, mouthparts, and the eight legs; and the **opisthosoma** or **abdomen**.

Carapace: The eyes are located on the anterior half of the carapace. Tarantulas, with very few exceptions, have eight eyes that are located on the eye tubercle or turret. We distinguish between anterior lateral eyes (ALE), anterior median eyes (AME), posterior median eyes (PME), and

ANATOMY OF A TARANTULA

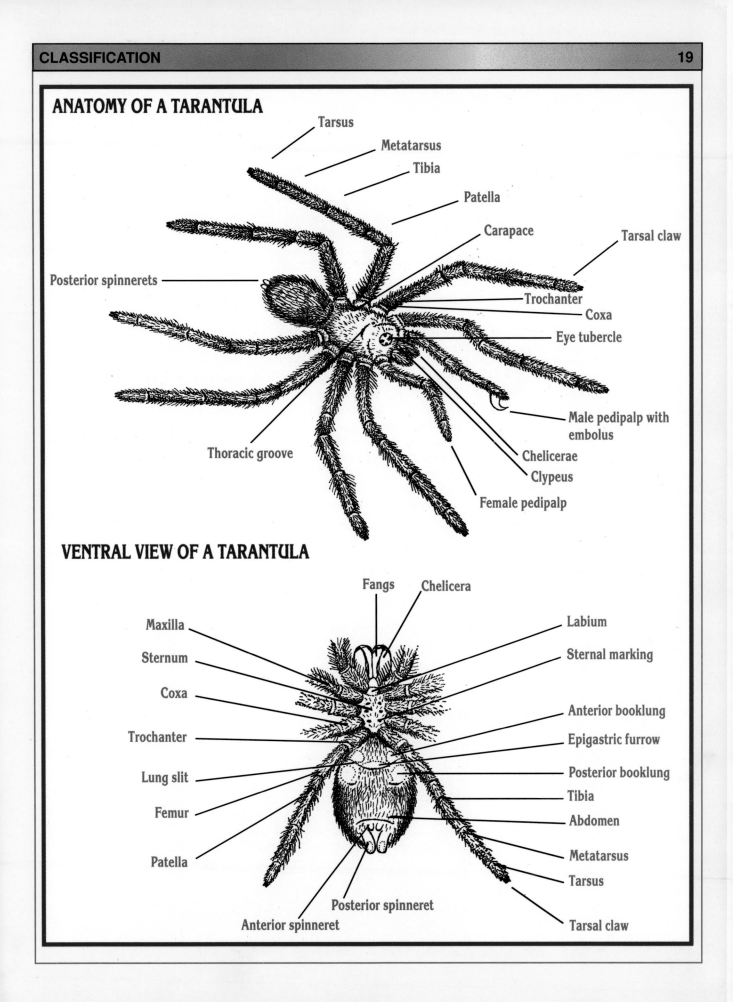

Tarsus

Metatarsus

Tibia

Patella

Carapace

Tarsal claw

Posterior spinnerets

Trochanter

Coxa

Eye tubercle

Male pedipalp with embolus

Thoracic groove

Chelicerae

Clypeus

Female pedipalp

VENTRAL VIEW OF A TARANTULA

Fangs

Chelicera

Maxilla

Labium

Sternum

Sternal marking

Coxa

Anterior booklung

Trochanter

Epigastric furrow

Lung slit

Posterior booklung

Femur

Tibia

Abdomen

Patella

Metatarsus

Tarsus

Posterior spinneret

Tarsal claw

Anterior spinneret

posterior lateral eyes (PLE). Their size and arrangement can be distinguishing characters. On the carapace there is a thoracic groove, an indentation in the thorax. This is the insertion point for the dorsal musculature of the underlying pumping stomach.

Sternum: The sternum, from an evolutionary perspective, developed from the fusion of four components. The labium is located near the mouth opening above the sternum. In addition, on the sternum there are sternal markings, which are used as distinguishing characters.

Chelicerae (fangs): The first pair of appendages on the prosoma are the chelicerae. They consist of a basal segment and a fang. Each part can be moved independently of the other. The venom gland is located in the basal segment. When the spider bites, it raises both fangs and rams them into the prey. The venom is injected at the same time. The basal segments also are equipped with cuticular teeth, which are helpful for macerating the prey.

Pedipalps and mouthparts: The pedipalps (often called the feelers and used much like an insect uses its antennae) are the second pair of appendages on the prosoma. Their segmentation is virtually the same as that of the legs, and they also are used for walking. In contrast to the legs, however, they have only six segments. In the adult male the last segment of the pedipalp, the tarsal segment, has become modified into a reproductive organ. The mouth opening is bordered laterally by the maxillae and posteriorly by the labium.

Legs: The legs arise like a fan from the soft-skinned connection between the carapace and sternum. Each leg has seven segments, which, from the body out, are in the following order: coxa, trochanter, femur, patella, tibia, metatarsus, and tarsus. On the tip of the tarsus are two tarsal claws, which usually are serrated and can be retracted. There are numerous sensory hairs on the legs.

Stridulatory organ: Some tarantula species are able to produce a hissing sound with the aid of bristles and spines. These may be located on the outside of the basal segment of the chelicera and on the coxa or on both, or on the trochanter of the pedipalp and the first two legs or both. Rubbing these areas together produces a faint sound; the process is called stridulation. The stridulatory organ is a distinguishing character because the arrangement can vary from species to species.

Opisthosoma: The

opisthosoma or abdomen is encased in an elastic covering that holds the heart, the midgut with its seven caeca, the booklungs, and the female sex organs. Furthermore, the spinnerets are attached to it.

THE MOLT

Tarantulas, like all spiders, are able to renew their exoskeleton at regular intervals. This process, called molting, represents a difficult stage in the spider's life. Outside the molting phases the prosoma and extremities are covered with a hard shell, the exocuticula, which does not permit growth. Growth can occur only in the few days following the molt, when the skeleton is still soft and elastic. In the time between the molting phases, the newly created cuticula forms under the actual skeleton, where it remains folded up.

The actual molting process usually is announced by the refusal to eat and the desire to hide. In bombardier spiders,

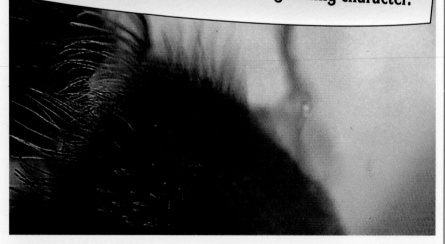

The stridulatory organ of *Grammostola spatulata*. With the stridulatory organ, tarantulas can produce hissing sounds. This organ varies from genus to genus and may be a good technical distinguishing character.

Sequence of photos showing a molt of *Brachypelma boehmei* with the regeneration of a lost leg. The molt is divided into three phases:

1. Splitting open of the prosoma.
2. Freeing of the opisthosoma.
3. Withdrawal of the extremities.

Pressure causes the cuticula to split open. This produces tension that causes the carapace to lift up like a lid. The abdomen is freed by means of tears originating in the cephalothorax.

After the molt the spider remains motionless for a fairly long time to recover from its exertions.

It takes several days before the exoskeleton of the spider hardens again. Growth occurs during this time.

which have brushed "bald spots" on their abdomen, an imminent molt is particularly easy to recognize. The bald spot turns black from the underlying skin color. When the molt is imminent most species spin a small web and then lie on their back to go through the molt in this position.

The actual molt is divided into three phases: splitting open of the prosoma, freeing of the opisthosoma, and pulling out of the extremities.

The splitting open of the cephalothorax (prosoma) begins with an increase in the heart rate. This causes more hemolymph (blood) to be pumped into the prosoma, which increases the weight of the prosoma by up to 80 percent, while the abdomen (opisthosoma) shrinks at the same time. The hemolymphic pressure produced in this way causes the cuticula to split. This splitting begins on the anterior and lateral parts of the cephalothorax. At the same time the forward-pointing chelicerae are moved up and down repeatedly to produce more tension. Finally the carapace is opened like a lid.

The freeing of the abdomen begins with the two tears extending from the cephalothorax to the abdomen. The skin of the abdomen, which has become wrinkled by the loss of hemolymph, is pulled off through the undulating contractions of the abdominal muscles.

While the aforementioned phase of the freeing of the abdomen continues, the extremities are simultaneously freed. This is the most difficult part of the molting process, when complications are the

most likely to arise. Whenever I have lost spiders during the molt, they were always in the phase when they were freeing the extremities. Through the increased hemolymphic pressure, the slightly wrinkled cuticula of the leg stretches, which causes the leg to bulge slightly out of the exuvia (skin). The exuvia is pushed out to the femur by the increase in pressure. After that, the shedding process is continued primarily by muscle contractions in the cephalothorax. In the process several legs remain motionless and the remaining legs work actively against them to free themselves. After the molt the spider stays motionless for half an hour or more to recover from its exertions. After this rest phase the spider begins, through "gymnastic" movements, to reestablish its leg function and finally "gets back on its feet again." The spider is still very soft and the chelicerae are white. It takes several days before the skeleton of the spider is completely hard again. Growth occurs during this time.

Males cease molting with the molt in which they develop sexual characters. In extremely rare cases it can happen that an adult male molts one more time. We do not know what factors trigger this abnormal molt, but it often happens that the male does not survive the second molt. If it gets through the second molt, however, the male is left with a deformed sperm bulb that makes copulation impossible.

The fascinating thing about a molt is the fact that many essential parts of the spider are replaced. If we examine closely an exuvia, we find, besides the

complete skeleton, the lenses of the eyes, the teeth at the base of the chelicerae, the pumping stomach, the booklungs, and, in females, the reproductive organs. If a leg or a spinneret was missing before the molt, it will be fully or partially regenerated during the molt. In a fully grown spider a single molt usually is not sufficient to regenerate full-sized legs. Often two to three molts are necessary for this. In juvenile spiders, however, full regeneration can occur in a single molt.

During the molt no food animals should be in the terrarium. These serve only to disturb the spider and even can nibble at it and cause great damage. Furthermore, the spider should, if possible, not be disturbed before, during, and after the molt. I still remember an alarmed caller who asked me to take a look at her "dying" tarantula, which already lay almost dead on its back. Ignorant hobbyists try repeatedly to stand the spider on its legs. The spider normally does not survive this disruption.

It has proved beneficial to raise the humidity in the terrarium before the molt. This measure seems to make the molt easier.

Several days after the molt, we can remove the exuvia (skin) from the terrarium. By then it is already hard and brittle. If we do not yet know the spider's sex, the exuvia can provide information on the matter. Do not discard the exuviae right away. If we plan to use the skin for decorative purposes, we can soften and unfold it again over steam. When nicely arranged, it looks deceptively like a real spider.

SEXING & REPRODUCTION

Distinguishing the sexes

Sex determination is an important topic, particularly if we intend to propagate tarantulas. If we want to distinguish the sexes of fully grown specimens and we have individuals of both sexes, the determination is relatively unproblematic. Adult males differ from females basically in that the tarsus of the pedipalp has been modified into a reproductive organ. This organ, as a rule, is folded and concealed in the hairs. Nonetheless, the complete scopula (fine hairs on the underside of the tarsus) is absent. This region is also thicker than in the female. The males of some species have tibial apophyses; one or two hook-like processes on the tibia of the first pair of legs. In some species the males are differently colored and even differently marked than the females. This is called sexual dimorphism or dichromatism. Examples of this are certain species of the genus *Poecilotheria* and the species *Aphonopelma seemanni*. The male of *Aphonopelma seemanni* differs so greatly in appearance from the female that no one knew what the males of this species looked like until subadult males underwent their adult molt in the terrarium. Previously, adult males of this species were erroneously classified as a separate species.

It can happen, however, that we do not know if the spiders whose sex we are to determine are already fully grown. In this case other characters come into play. There are two possible approaches here. On the one hand we can examine a shed skin or exuvia; on the other we can examine the structures and forms of the region around the epigastric furrow (reproductive opening in spiders).

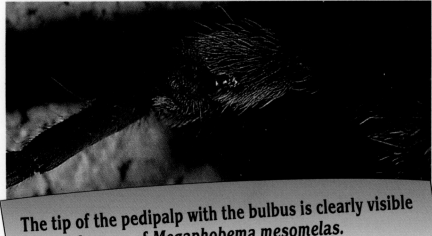

The tip of the pedipalp with the bulbus is clearly visible in this close-up of *Megaphobema mesomelas*.

The safest method is the examination of an exuvia. If it is a female, the exuvia must exhibit a spermatheca or seminal receptacle (sperm sac). We find this by softening and unfolding the skin of the abdomen so that we can look at the inner side of the skin from above. The first orientation points are the four booklungs, which are white and stand out from the brown skin of the abdomen. If the specimen is a female, the spermatheca will be located in the center of these four lungs, displaced slightly in the direction of the cephalothorax. The form of the spermatheca can vary depending on the genus and species. It varies from a simple, flat tubercle to a complicated, intertwined or even cauliflower-like structure. If a spermatheca is present in the exuvia, the specimen is a female. The spermatheca already is present in juveniles but is more difficult to find, and we certainly cannot see it without a stereomicroscope and a fine dissecting needle.

The other method of sex determination consists of the evaluation of the structure and form of the area of the epigastric furrow from the outside. This method is easy to carry out, because it requires no aid or apparatus. A good eye is all we need.

Anterior to the female's reproductive opening is the

epigynum, which is a slightly raised region in front of the actual epigastric furrow. This raised area is visible when we observe the spider's abdomen from the side. Also, on the underside of the abdomen two lines extend from the transition to the cephalothorax to the epigastric furrow. Experience has shown that the lines form a trapezoid in the female, but only a normal rectangle in the male. In the male there often is a spot in this rectangle. In *Avicularia minatrix* this spot is characteristic.

The larger the spider on which this method of sex determination is used, the greater the chances that the determination will be successful. It occasionally happens, however, that such a determination yields a false result. Particularly with smaller species and subadult specimens of the genus *Avicularia*, the characters often are weakly developed and hard to see. The safest method is to examine whether or not the exuvia of a spider has a spermatheca.

Mating and breeding

When we have a sexually mature pair of a species, any tarantula keeper will be tempted to breed the species. Every successful captive breeding makes it unnecessary to take specimens from the wild. This ensures that a number of years from now these species will continue to be kept in our terraria, particularly since the importation of species from many countries in the world is being sharply restricted through export bans.

The overwhelming majority of tarantula species are easy to breed as long as we consider a few fundamental points. Before mating them, however, we should be aware of the consequences should breeding be successful. Many species are very productive and produce several hundred spiderlings at a time. Of *Lasiodora parahybana* we know that approximately 1200 spiderlings have emerged from a cocoon. Although we will initially be happy to see an abundance of offspring, we will begin to have our doubts when it is time to feed the spiderlings. Juveniles also tend to be quite difficult to sell at meetings or to the pet trade, and we often cannot find enough takers for all the offspring. Not infrequently the young spiders are used as food for lizards or frogs or are kept together, which leads to a natural decimation through cannibalism. Therefore, before any breeding attempt we must consider if, following a successful breeding, we have the necessary time to care for the spiderlings and provide them with the necessary amounts of food. Furthermore, we need suitable terraria and sufficient space to set them up.

Before any mating can take place, we should consider several factors.

The female should not be approaching a molt. On the one hand, in all likelihood the female would not mate with the male, and if she did, the mating would be in vain, because in the molt following the mating the female genitalia would also be shed and the sperm would remain in the old skin. Therefore, we should

only mate females that have molted relatively recently. If a female is ready to molt, we should wait until it is completed. A mating can be attempted approximately six to eight weeks after the molt.

After the male undergoes the last molt, we must wait until it builds a sperm web. The male's sperm is located in the abdomen and emerges in the epigastric furrow. The male must first "load" the sperm into the bulbs to perform copulation. For this purpose the male builds a sperm web of silk that it fastens at two points like a hammock. To attach the sperm to the sperm web, the male crawls under it. Subsequently, he climbs over the web and draws the sperm into the bulbs. Only now is the male able to transfer the sperm to the female's seminal receptacles during copulation. It takes some luck to observe the male during the construction of the sperm web, because the process takes only a few hours. Subsequently, however, the torn web, the remnants of the "hammock," remains on the bottom, which indicates that the sperm are in the bulbs. It can take approximately six to ten weeks after the last molt before the male "loads" its bulbs for the first time. After a successful copulation this procedure usually is repeated because the empty bulbs must be refilled.

If we now have two ready-to-breed spiders, we must select the terrarium in which mating is to take place. If the female's terrarium is large enough, it is best to have the mating take place there. A terrarium with an area of 40 x 40 centimeters

The respective bulbs of:

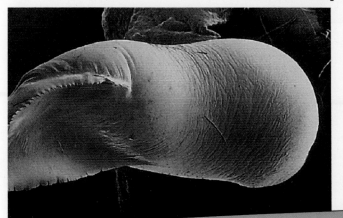 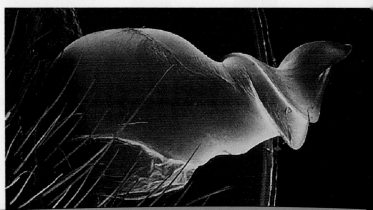

Theraphosa leblondi

Poecilotheria fasciata

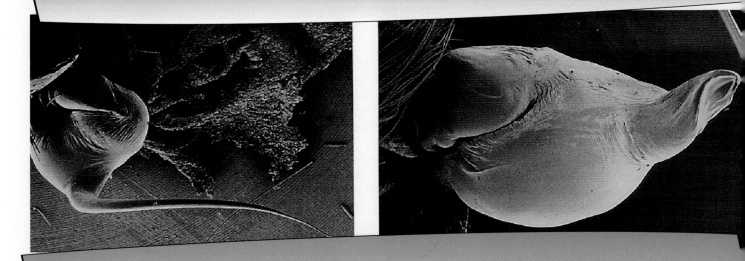

Avicularia minatrix

Brachypelma smithi

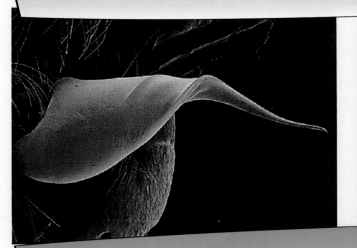 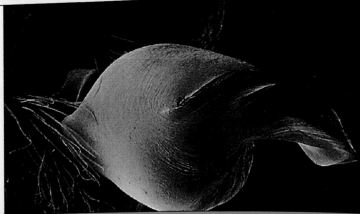

Grammostola argentinensis

Cyclosternum fasciatum

(16 x 16 inches) or larger is sufficient. With arboreal species the terrarium height should be at least 40 centimeters (16 inches). A terrarium of this size gives the male the opportunity to withdraw from the female if the female is not ready to breed and possibly reacts aggressively toward the male. In my opinion, mating should take place in the female's terrarium because this corresponds most closely to the natural conditions. In the wild, the female always stays in the same den. Mature males wander during the breeding season and visit the females in their dens. The females also spin special threads near their dens that signal to the male that the female is ready to mate.

If the female's terrarium is too small for breeding, we can set up and furnish a terrarium specifically for breeding. This terrarium does not have to be specially furnished except that a den must be present with terrestrial species. We then put the female in the terrarium one to two weeks before breeding to give her time to become acclimated to her new surroundings and to spin her threads with the pheromones to signal males her mating readiness.

If the external conditions for a mating are present, the big event can take place. When a species breeds for the first time, we cannot predict if the mating will be peaceful. Therefore, we should observe the mating with long forceps or a wooden rod so we can come to the male's aid if the female attacks him.

In my experience, the time of day has no influence on mating, although matings in the wild predominantly occur at night. The reason for this is that both the males and females usually do not dare to leave their hole or hiding place during the day, because they would be highly vulnerable to their predators.

Mating begins when we put the male in the female's terrarium, as far from the female's den as possible. As a rule, the male, depending on the species, begins to jerk or even to tremble with his whole body and sometimes to drum with his legs or pedipalps. The female detects these vibrations and usually is induced to leave her den or to drum on the substrate with her pedipalps and first pair of legs, or both. This reaction by the female usually is a good sign and signals her readiness to breed. The male usually reacts to the female's drumming with drumming of his own. When the male is close enough to the female, he palpates the female's front legs, cautiously at first and then more and more vigorously. This further stimulates the female and induces her to rear up. This is necessary because the male must be able to reach the underside of the female's abdomen with his pedipalps. So as not to be endangered unnecessarily while he is under the female, the male raises the female with his first pair of legs by placing them between the female's spread chelicerae. If the male has tibial apophyses, he hooks them into the female's chelicerae. In this way the male is able to lift the female and to maintain a firm hold on her. Next, the male attempts to insert one of his bulbs into the female's epigastric furrow. As a sign for the successful insertion of the bulb, the female bends sharply, because the male pulls the female's abdomen toward him while he transfers the semen. When copulation is complete, the male releases his hold and walks away from the female.

The version described above represents an optimal course of events. Various disruptions can occur, however, that delay mating or even make it impossible. If the female is not ready to breed, she will not respond to the male's courtship signals. If the male approaches the female, and the female has not signaled her readiness to breed, this can be a life-threatening situation for the male. If the female does not recognize the male as a male, he is automatically considered as prey and is captured. Because males have a more delicate build, they usually have no chance to defend themselves against the female. Often their only option is to escape. It also can happen that the female will attack the male immediately after mating. Here we should intervene with the forceps or wooden rod to come to the male's assistance.

To be certain that the female has actually mated, we can wait until the male has constructed a new sperm web and copulates again.

Some species are very peaceful during mating and can be kept together for a fairly long time in a sufficiently large terrarium. This may last for several weeks. Fundamentally, this is more true of arboreal than of terrestrial species. Nonetheless, there are

Spermatheca of :

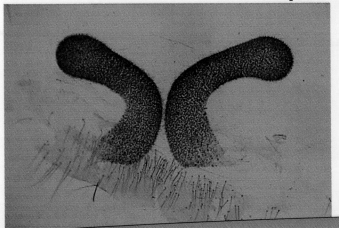

Avicularia avicularia

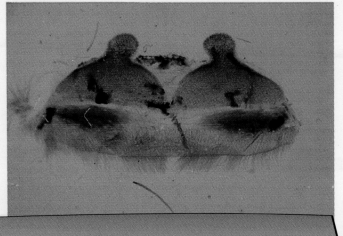

Aphonopelma seemani

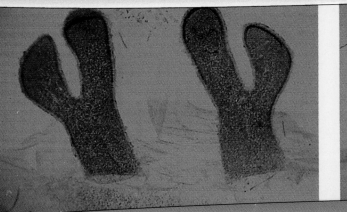

Citharischius crawshayi

Grammostola spatulata

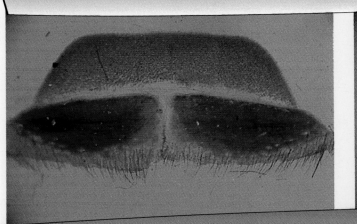

Brachypelma smithi

Paraphysa pulcherrimaklassi

exceptions to this rule. With species of the genus *Poecilotheria*, for example, it can happen that the male will be eaten after one or several copulations. On the other hand, in my experience species of the genera *Avicularia, Psalmopoeus,* *Tapinauchenius, Pachistopelma,* and *Stromatoplema* definitely can be kept together for several weeks and the male subsequently removed uninjured from the terrarium. I do not want to make any guarantees here, however, because in exceptional cases it can happen that the male will fall prey to the female, particularly when the male is already fairly old.

My experiences have shown that unmated males live considerably longer than their mated conspecifics. When a

A. Underside of a female *Acanthoscurria* sp. from Uruguay.

C. Underside of a subadult male of *Acanthoscurria* sp. from Uruguay.

B. Underside of a female of *Acanthoscurria* sp. from Uruguay.

D. Underside of a subadult male of *Acanthoscurria* sp. from Uruguay.

A mating sequence of *Pamphobeteus* sp. from Ecuador. The breeding of tarantulas certainly is a great attraction for any hobbyist, for it proves that the spiders are being kept under optimal conditions. Because it is not always easy to find homes for young spiders, however, we must consider beforehand whether breeding seems to make sense.

male has recently molted and the female is almost ready to molt, we should not rush events. As a rule, the male will be old enough to wait for a favorable time for both sexes to mate. In individual cases adult males have lived for up to four years.

After a successful mating, the female will behave completely normally for a while. She will merely have a bigger appetite and develop a larger abdomen. Because the sperm are stored in the female's body, it can take

A male *Megaphobema mesomelas* showing a tibial apophysis on one of the legs. Males with tibial apophyses can hook them onto the female's chelicerae, which makes it possible to lift the female and to get a firmer grip during mating.

some time before cocoon building begins. We do not yet know precisely what factors trigger cocoon construction in the terrarium. In the wild, climatic changes of the seasons usually trigger cocoon construction. In the terrarium we can simulate such a climatic change if the female shows no inclination to

build a cocoon for a fairly long time. We need to show some patience, however, because cocoon construction can still occur a year or more following mating.

The building of a cocoon usually is announced by the refusal to eat. After that the female begins to spin herself into her den or tree nest. If she is a bombardier spider that has brushed the hairs from her abdomen, at this stage we cannot tell if the spider is molting or is building a cocoon. The female

often spins such a dense web that we cannot see inside the nest. All we can do now is wait, for if the spider is molting, she will reappear in a few days. If this is not the case, we can assume that the spider has built a cocoon.

The actual construction of the cocoon begins with the spinning of a dense, round

web. The eggs are laid on this platform and are fertilized as they emerge from the body. After that, the female rolls the eggs in the previously spun web and spins more silk around the web until she has created a spherical structure. The female usually guards this cocoon until the spiderlings emerge. When the female recognizes, however, that something is wrong with the cocoon or it has been disturbed, she tears it open or simply abandons it. Some breeders believe that we should remove the cocoon from the female after about four to six weeks because the movements caused by the hatching spiderlings can induce the female to eat the cocoon. I disagree with this opinion because I do not believe that the spiderlings' movements induce the mother to eat the cocoon. Rather, in my opinion other factors are of decisive importance, such as that the eggs are infertile or that incorrect external conditions in the terrarium have led to the loss of the cocoon. For this reason I leave the spiderlings with the mother until just before they emerge. Depending on the external conditions and the species, this can take 7 to 12 weeks. An imminent hatching is announced by the mother spider beginning to loosen the cocoon to provide more space for the spiderlings. This makes the cocoon larger and fluffier. I usually remove it during this phase. I do not do this because I am afraid that the female might eat it; rather, it is considerably easier if the spiderlings emerge in a separate container than when they

Spiderlings of *Pterinochilus* sp. after the second molt in the cocoon.

have to be removed individually from the terrarium. We must provide some obstetrics care if we remove the cocoon from the mother spider. This consists of carefully cutting a slit in the cocoon with fine scissors to make it possible for the spiderlings to emerge.

I store cocoons that I have removed from the mother before hatching in a clean plastic container, the bottom of which I cover with damp paper towels. It is best to put the container in a location with a temperature of about 25°C (77°). We should keep the paper towels moist at all times.

Rearing young tarantulas

After the spiderlings emerge, we must transfer them individually to suitable containers. Although it usually takes a few weeks before cannibalism begins, we should not wait this long. Very small spiderlings, such as those of *Cyriocosmus elegans,* a very attractive dwarf tarantula species, can be housed in plastic film containers. The spiderlings are only about 2 to 3 millimeters (less than an eighth of an inch) long, and these containers provide more than enough space. Somewhat larger spiderlings, such as those of *Brachypelma emilia,* which are about 8 millimeters (0.33 inch) long, can be put in *Drosophila* jars. These jars are clear and are sealed with a foam plug that is permeable to air. Normally *Drosophila,* that is, fruitflies, are bred in them. These jars are available in various sizes and can be purchased from dealers and biological supply houses. For the larger specimens of

spiderlings, such as those of *Theraphosa leblondi* or *Pamphobeteus fortis,* we can house them in plastic containers. As the spiderlings grow, we must, of course, increase correspondingly the size of container. When the spiderlings have become juveniles, that is, are half grown, and have become too large for plastic containers,

to subadult spiders, the smaller sizes have proved particularly useful. Larger sizes can be considered as terraria for fully grown specimens.

Once we have properly housed the spiderlings, we must consider that in the first place a young spider needs more care than a fully grown spider. This is particularly

Pamphobeteus platyomma with her cocoon. The construction of a cocoon usually is announced by a refusal to eat. The female withdraws into her den to spin the cocoon.

small plastic terraria can be used. We can use these terraria until the spiders are large enough to put into the terrarium that will house them permanently. These terraria are offered in various sizes and have a clear body and a fluted cover (usually with a lid that can be lifted for feeding) that is permeable to air. For juvenile

true of moisture, which should always be present in the terrarium. The temperature must not exceed 28°C (82°F). Even a short period of drying out can lead to the death of the young spider. When feeding, we must make sure that the size of the food animal is appropriate for the spiderling. Although it often happens that young spiders capture food animals that are larger than themselves, as a rule we should offer food that is at most the same size. Some young spiders avoid larger food animals and only capture prey that is smaller than themselves. If possible, we should observe the reaction of the spiderling to the food animal. If the food animal is the same size or larger than the spider, and if the spider does not capture the food animal within a few hours, we should remove the food animal and replace it with a smaller one. In exceptional cases it can happen that the food animal will attack the spider. This happens primarily when it is considerably larger than the spider.

We can assume that the better the conditions under which the spiderling is kept, the faster it will grow. This means that if we provide warmth, moisture, and an abundant food supply, the spiderling will flourish. A few species, such as *Psalmopoeus cambridgei*, can grow to the adult stage within a year. Nonetheless, experience has shown that not all spiderlings from the same cocoon grow at the same rate under the same conditions. There are always a few specimens that grown considerably larger than their siblings. As we usually discover later, the first specimens to reach maturity usually are males. Why this is so is not known. It becomes a problem, however, when we only have juveniles from the same cocoon and we wish to breed the species. When the males are already mature, the females often need several more months or longer to

reach the adult stage. To overcome this problem, we must try to determine the sexes at an early stage. When we have separated the males, we can rear them under somewhat cooler conditions and offer them less food. In this way we can get each sex to reach maturity at about the same time.

I often have noticed that hobbyists avoid acquiring spiderlings because of the fear of losses. This fear, however, is unfounded in the majority of cases. As long as we consider the aforementioned measures, in most cases nothing can happen. It is true that we must expect more losses with juveniles than with adults. When I hear of large losses in the rearing of spiderlings, I often have the feeling that the keeper is working too much with them. This may sound paradoxical at first, but in my opinion these animals can suffer from stress. When the

young spiders are offered food every day and the humidity is checked each day, this means daily stress for the spiders. I always stick to a 14-day routine in caring for my juveniles. Although the juveniles do not grow as fast as when they are fed almost daily, the metabolism also is not as rapid, which subsequently affects the life-expectancy.

I advise anyone who must choose between acquiring a wild-caught spider and a captive-bred specimen to take the captive-bred spider. As a rule, captive-bred specimens are healthier than wild-caught spiders. Juveniles can be purchased more cheaply and the keeper also can take pleasure in watching them grow. Another important aspect is that if we acquire captive-bred specimens, we do not have to take spiders from the wild.

A plastic terrarium suitable for rearing spiderlings. These small plastic terraria offer sufficient space to rear young tarantulas successfully. Cleaning and care in a plastic terrarium of this kind are very simple.

DISEASES & INJURIES

DISEASES AND INJURIES

The diseases and injuries of tarantulas are very difficult topics because we have no experiences, certain diagnoses, or effective therapies. Often the spiders simply refuse to eat and die after some time from apparent illness. Injuries, on the other hand, are somewhat more treatable, and we occasionally can prevent the death of a spider.

Some of the few clinical pictures that are visible externally are swellings, discolorations, and abrasions on the skin of the abdomen. Discolorations are visible only with bombardier spiders with brushed-off hairs. Swellings that form on the abdomen always are clearly visible. In my experience, however, we can do nothing about them. It can happen that the condition will improve following several molts. I, at least, am unaware of any effective therapy. I have owned a few spiders, however, in which the swellings of the abdomen later disappeared.

We can do more with injuries. For example, let's say that a spider breaks a leg in a fall. The hemolymph then flows out of the break. If we do nothing about it, the part either breaks off in an uncontrolled manner or may grow back deformed. It is therefore advisable to amputate part of the leg. The best place to do this is the next leg segment between the break and the body. In this place we should cut through the leg between the segments with a scalpel or sharp scissors. This is not something that everyone is willing to do, but it does promote the healing process. A clean break also reduces the likelihood of complications appearing at the next molt. Following the amputation, we should treat the open wound with a little spray dressing; cover the rest of the spider to keep it from being sprayed. For this purpose we can cut a small hole in a piece of cardboard through which we can spray the wound at a suitable distance. If the spider does not keep still, then please follow the instructions described in the chapter on handling tarantulas.

An injury to the abdomen is far more difficult to heal. Although we can use a spray dressing or petroleum jelly to stop the outflow of hemolymph, the chances of healing are much reduced. If the abdominal tear is large, I would put the spider in the freezer to prevent further suffering. This certainly is the best way to euthanize a tarantula. We can treat smaller tears as described above, although the chances of success are quite uncertain. Ultimately, the spider may also have suffered other internal injuries. I therefore must repeatedly appeal to keepers not to remove their spiders unnecessarily from their terrarium. Terrestrial species in particular are in more danger because they can suffer life-threatening injuries even in a fall from a low height.

We can treat other injuries, such as damage to the cephalothorax, injuries to or loss of the chelicerae, and so forth, only by stopping the bleeding. Unfortunately, we must leave the rest to nature.

Dead tarantulas usually retract their legs under their body. When we find dead specimens, they usually are in this position. Should we find a spider in this condition, close attention is required. Should the terrarium have dried out for some reason, it may be beneficial to put the tarantula in a filled water dish (assuming, of course, that it really is not dead). In this way it can take up water, and if this was the reason it dried out, it soon will recover. Often it is improper keeping conditions that hobbyists provide out of ignorance that can lead to large losses. For example, for a long time hobbyists kept specimens of the genus *Eucratoscelus* under much too dry conditions. It would be easy to assume that animals from central Africa would not need a particularly moist living space. The fact is, however, that these spiders excavate very deep dens, and the soil is very moist at a certain depth. After a number of attempts it turned out that it is best to keep *Eucratoscelus* in a large preserving jar filled three-quarters full with moist soil and always covered. Although the ventilation is very weak, scarcely any humidity can escape. Many Asian terrestrial species are also best kept in this way.

IRRITATING HAIRS

Another important topic is the irritating hairs that certain tarantulas (which often are called bombardier spiders) use as a defensive mechanism. Many hobbyists have had to give up their tarantulas because they had problems with irritating hairs. I personally know of a case in which the keeper suffered from a skin rash, difficulty in breathing, and swelling and even deformation of body parts when he came into contact with irritating hairs of species of the genus *Avicularia*. Opening the terrarium was enough to produce the symptoms, as a few irritating hairs were swirled through the air.

Tarantulas use these irritating hairs to repel predators. When threatened, the terrestrial species turn around in their den and send a cloud of irritating hairs toward the intruder. A rodent, for example, that has had such an experience will be reluctant to pursue a tarantula in the future.

Arboreal species line their silk webs with these irritating hairs to provide protection against predators. Therefore, we should avoid touching the silk webs of arboreal species with our bare hands. A pair of rubber gloves offers good protection.

If we examine irritating hairs under the microscope, we can see tiny hooks that make it difficult to remove the hairs from the skin. Often merely washing the hands after an attack is not enough to relieve the itching. Soft parts of the skin, such as between the fingers, are particularly sensitive. Mucous membranes, however, also can swell. Basically, each person reacts differently to irritating hairs. Fortunately, in most keepers the physical reaction is limited to itching.

As I said, not all tarantula species have irritating hairs. It is primarily the New World species from South and Central America that repel predators with this behavior.

A number of genera whose species are equipped with irritating hairs are popular in our terraria. These include *Brachypelma*, *Pamphobeteus*, *Theraphosa*, *Pseudotheraphosa*, *Sericopelma*, *Lasiodora*, *Grammostola*, *Phormictopus*, and *Avicularia*. It is easy to recognize if a particular species is a bombardier spider. All we need to do is to annoy the spider a little. If it starts to brush its hind legs against its abdomen, this is conclusive proof that it is a bombardier spider.

Pamphobeteus antinous with a "bald spot." This defensive reaction can cause unpleasant itching in the keeper.

ARE THEY DANGEROUS?

A great deal of false information has been reported on the toxic nature of tarantulas. Unfortunately, it is repeatedly reported, particularly in the sensational press, that tarantulas have killed people with their deadly venom. Often it also is said that these persons had been "stung," through which we can immediately recognize the incompetence of the authors. The truth is that there is no known tarantula whose bite can kill a healthy adult. There certainly are spiders whose bites can be fatal to human beings. Among these are the black widows (*Latrodectus*) and certain other comb-footed spiders. Tarantulas, however, do not belong to this group.

The fact is that the venom of tarantulas has a weak effect on warm-blooded animals. In reptiles, on the other hand, the toxic effect is considerably stronger. The venom of tarantulas consists of various polypeptides and apparently has a neurotoxic effect.

I myself have never been bitten by a tarantula, although I am familiar with cases among my circle of acquaintances. In one case a 23-year-old was bitten by a *Brachypelma vagans* on the tip of the right index finger.

The toxic effect was so slight that the victim was able to continue his daily activities without impairment. In another case the same person, while photographing a *Hysterocrates hercules,* was bitten on the instep of the right foot. The result was a local reddening of the skin, a tingling in the affected foot, and later slight cramp-like symptoms of paralysis in the right leg. The symptoms continued for several days.

Experience has shown that Asian and African tarantula species are more "poisonous" than New World species. It is known, for example, that bites of *Poecilotheria* species and *Pterinochilus* species can lead to strong reddening of the skin and symptoms of paralysis. The physical reactions to a tarantula bite, however, vary from individual to individual. If the bitten person is allergic to tarantula venom, serious symptoms can appear.

Basically, we should handle tarantulas so that the spider never has the opportunity to bite. Should we happen to be bitten, the most important thing is to remain calm. The wound usually will be painful, which is mainly due to the mechanical effect of the chelicerae. As long as the circulation remains stable and no other symptoms appear, it usually is sufficient to disinfect the wound and, if necessary, to get a tetanus shot. If problems occur, we should go to a doctor, who usually will treat them symptomatically. Sera for the treatment of tarantula bites do not exist because they are unnecessary.

In the meantime, the pharmaceutical industry has discovered and used tarantula venom. In Australia, for example, the venom is used to manufacture sleeping pills. These sleeping pills have the advantage that their effect does not decrease; even after taking them for a long time a higher dosage is unnecessary. Medicines of this kind, however, have not yet been approved. A number of scientists are currently working with tarantula venom. They have developed an apparatus to "milk" tarantulas, such as has been done for a long time with snakes. The venom obtained in this way is mainly used for analysis, because the composition of the venom of most tarantula species still is unknown.

COMMON TARANTULAS

In the following section, with text and illustrations, I would like to present a number of tarantulas that have already made their appearance in our terraria, pointing out the special features that distinguish the particular species. The species are in alphabetical order.

Acanthoscurria antillensis
Pocock 1903
Provenance: Lesser Antilles
Terrestrial species

The species reaches a body size of about 6 centimeters (2.4 inches). The ground color of this tarantula is brown with a coppery metallic sheen on the cephalothorax and legs. The area of the terrarium should be about 30 x 30 centimeters (12 x 12 inches). A deep substrate is beneficial, because the species is an avid and deep digger. *A. antillensis* is easy to breed and produces approximately 300 to 400 spiderlings. We can describe the species as slightly aggressive. Before the molt the tarantulas are pale brown, but they have a dark-brown color after the molt.

Aphonopelma chalcodes
Chamberlin 1939
Provenance: United States, Mexico
Terrestrial species

Aphonopelma chalcodes attains a body length of about 6 to 7 centimeters (2.4 to 2.8 inches). Individuals of this species are pale beige on the cephalothorax and legs and brown on the abdomen. A terrarium for this species should have an area of 30 x 30 centimeters (12 x 12 inches). This species makes no special demands in its keeping requirements, although a not too humid climate has proved effective. I have no information on reproduction, but the species has been bred in captivity. The tarantulas generally have a peaceful temperament. Fully grown specimens in particular are highly coveted because they are seldom available on the market.

Aphonopelma seemani
Cambridge 1897
Provenance: Costa Rica to Texas and California
Terrestrial species

This species generally reaches a body length of 6 centimeters (2.4 inches). There are several variations in coloration. Some individuals have a nearly pale brown ground color, while others are leaden gray with an in part nearly bluish suffusion. The colors of the stripes on the patellae also

Acanthoscurria antillensis, male. This tarantula species can be slightly aggressive and tends to dig extensively in the terrarium.

Aphonopelma chalcodes, female. The terrarium for this species should have a minimum area of 30 x 30 centimeters (12 x 12 inches). This species is much in demand but seldom is offered on the market.

Aphonopelma seemani, female. In coloration there are a number of variants ranging from light brown to gray-blue. This species is undemanding but hard to breed. Wild-caught females are well-suited for breeding.

vary in intensity. We should house this species in a terrarium with an area of 30 x 30 centimeters (12 x 12 inches). This species does not make any special demands with respect to keeping requirements. The species seems to be quite difficult to breed, because the males are usually very nervous and run away at the female's slightest movement. There are very few reports of offspring resulting from matings in the terrarium. Most offspring resulted from wild-caught females. This species exhibits sexual dimorphism; the adult males lose the species-typical markings and coloration after the last molt and subsequently are a uniform dark brown.

Avicularia metallica
Ausserer 1875

Provenance: Surinam to northern Brazil
Arboreal species

This species attains a body length of about 5 to 6 centimeters (2 to 2.4 inches). It is black in color and can exhibit pale red or beige hairs on the legs. On the cephalothorax, in particular, there is a metallic blue sheen that gives the species its name. The terrarium should have an area of about 25 x 25 centimeters (10 x 10 inches) and a height of 30 centimeters (12 inches). This species is quite easy to keep. We should always keep the substrate moist and we should spray the terrarium twice a week. The species has been bred frequently in captivity. Even so, fully grown specimens, in particular, are in great

demand because of their peaceful temperament. They are rather good climbers and constantly sense the environment with their pedipalps as they walk. As a rule, a cocoon contains from 70 to 150 spiderlings. Mating usually goes off without complications. Because well-fed females normally are not aggressive toward the males, we usually can safely keep the male for several weeks in the female's terrarium. This species is often offered on the market under the name *Avicularia avicularia*.

Avicularia minatrix Pocock 1903
Provenance: Venezuela
Arboreal species

This is one of the smaller members of the genus *Avicularia*. Females usually reach a body length of about 3 to 4 centimeters (1.2 to 1.6 inches). This tarantula is pink and brown in color and as an adult retains the striped markings on the abdomen that it also exhibits in the juvenile stage. Because the tarantulas are not too large, a terrarium with the dimensions 20 x 20 x 25 centimeters (8 x 8 x 10 inches)(length x width x height) is adequate. The furnishings should include cork tubes with a small diameter, because in the wild the tarantulas prefer to live in hollow trees or branches as well as in bromeliads. We must avoid keeping conditions that are too moist. It is completely adequate if we keep just the substrate moist. This species has been bred repeatedly in captivity, and, as a rule, the rearing of the spiderlings also presents no problems. Unfortunately,

the cocoons often contain only 30 to 40 spiderlings. These tarantulas have an absolutely peaceful temperament. A peculiarity of the species that hobbyists have reported to me is that if we give it enough space and food, we can keep several individuals in the same terrarium. I, however, have never tried this.

Avicularia purpurea Kirk 1990
Provenance: Ecuador
Arboreal species

This species reaches approximately the same body size as *Avicularia metallica*, namely about 5 centimeters (2 inches). It also has a black ground color, but the tarantulas have a deep lilac suffusion on the legs and the cephalothorax, which has given this species its name. The terrarium size should be about 25 x 25 x 30 centimeters (10 x 10 x 12 inches)(length x width x height). We should keep the substrate moist and spray the terrarium twice a week. Provide good ventilation in the terrarium. The tarantulas live in the wild primarily in tree crevices and knotholes. These conditions are easy to mimic with pieces of cork bark. With this species mating is without problems and we can keep the male with the female for a fairly long time. As a rule, a cocoon contains from 70 to 120 spiderlings that, in contrast to most other *Avicularia* species, have black and white markings. Although specimens of this species usually have a good disposition, if you annoy them for a fairly long time they can become aggressive.

Avicularia metallica, female. The metallic blue sheen gives this tarantula its name. This species is in great demand with beginners because of its peaceful temperament.

Avicularia minatrix, female. This species grows only 3 to 4 centimeters (1.2 to 1.6 inches) long and therefore does well in a fairly small terrarium.

Avicularia versicolor
(Walckenaer 1837)
Provenance: Martinique, Guadeloupe
Arboreal species

This species reaches a body size of approximately 5 to 6 centimeters (2 to 2.4 inches). It probably is one of the most beautiful members of the genus *Avicularia*. As a juvenile it is steel blue with a striped abdomen. In adults the cephalothorax is also steel blue, but the legs and abdomen are brownish pink. The terrarium size with this species should be 25 x 25 x 30 centimeters (10 x 10 x 12 inches)(length x width x height). It is easy to keep. Here, too, it is sufficient to keep the substrate moist. With breeding, however, you should exercise somewhat more caution with this species, because the usual method of keeping the male with the female for a fairly long time often ends with the female eating the male. This does not necessarily mean that mating does not occur, but the male naturally will no longer be available for further breeding attempts. Therefore, with this species I advise returning the male to its own terrarium after mating. A cocoon of this species normally contains approximately 80 to 160 spiderlings, which are easy to rear. *A. versicolor* has a peaceful disposition and normally is not aggressive.

Avicularia purpurea, female. This species likes a moist substrate, therefore we must spray the terrarium at least twice a week. In the wild they live in crevices in trees, under tree bark, and in knot holes.

Avicularia versicolor. This is one of the most beautiful species of the genus *Avicularia.* It is very easy to keep as long as we make sure that the substrate is moist. We should spray the terrarium twice a week.

Avicularia versicolor, juvenile. This tarantula species has a peaceful disposition and is not aggressive. Nonetheless, caution is advised before and during mating, because the female has a tendency to eat the male. We must return the male to his own terrarium immediately after mating. In this photograph you can see that this is a very beautiful tarantula, which readily explains its popularity.

Brachypelma albopilosa
Valerio 1980
Provenance: Costa Rica
Terrestrial species

This species attains a body length of approximately 6 to 7 centimeters (2.4 to 2.8 inches). It is very popular with many hobbyists and particularly with beginners because of its attractive appearance and very peaceful disposition. This tarantula has a brown ground color with a gold suffusion on the cephalothorax. Its legs and abdomen are strewn with frizzy hairs. We should house this tarantula in a terrarium with an area of about 30 x 30 centimeters (12 x 12 inches). Breeding usually is unproblematic. A cocoon contains several hundred spiderlings that are only a few millimeters long at hatching. The juveniles also grow relatively slowly, and they require at least two to three years to reach maturity. Because of the large number of spiderlings per cocoon, the tarantulas often are available at low prices, which means that the species is not often bred in captivity. In the meantime the species has become somewhat less common.

Brachypelma auratum
Schmidt 1992
Provenance: Mexico
Terrestrial species

B. auratum is a medium-sized species and reaches a body length of 5 centimeters (2 inches). It is similar in color to *B. smithi,* and for a long time it was considered to be the "highland form" of *B. smithi. B. auratum* also has a red marking on the patellae of the legs. It is dark red, however, not orange as in *B. smithi.* The individual leg joints under the patella are a contrasting pale color. The tarantula generally has a somewhat darker overall ground color than *B. smithi.* The cephalothorax also has a pale border. The abdomen is dark with scattered red-brown hairs. We should keep *B. auratum* in a terrarium with an area of 30 x 30 centimeters (12 x 12 inches).

Brachypelma albopilosa, male.

Brachypelma albopilosa, female. This tarantula species is highly recommended for beginners because it is very peaceful, easy to keep, and very attractively colored.

The species does not make any special demands with respect to keeping requirements, but the conditions should be on the dry side. I have no information on breeding. Although offspring have been bred in captivity, I do not know if they were produced in captive matings (i.e., they could have come from gravid wild-caught females). To my knowledge there is a shortage of males for breeding. *B. auratum* has a peaceful temperament but is one of the bombardier spiders.

Brachypelma boehmei
G. Schmidt & P. Klaas 1993
Provenance: Mexico
Terrestrial species

B. boehmei grows somewhat larger than *B. albopilosa* and attains a body length of about 6 to 7 centimeters (2.4 to 2.8 inches). Its coloration is striking. The patella, tibia, and metatarsus of the leg are orange and the cephalothorax is pale beige. The femur and the abdomen are black, although the abdomen exhibits some beige-colored hairs. The species is new and was not described until 1993. The terrarium should have an area of 30 x 30 centimeters (12 x 12 inches). *B. boehmei* makes no special demands in regard to keeping requirements. On the contrary, because the tarantulas come from a region in Mexico with a fairly long dry period, they readily tolerate an arid climate in the terrarium. That does not mean, however, that we should keep the tarantulas without moisture. Breeding

also is quite easy here and the tarantulas do not act aggressively toward each other. On the contrary, during mating they do not appear to react to external conditions, because they also mate undisturbed outside the terrarium. A cocoon of this species contains 600 or more spiderlings. Although this tarantula is peaceful, as are all *Brachypelma* species, it is one of the bombardier spiders. *B. boehme* is particularly nervous, and at the slightest disturbance it starts to brush off the hairs of the abdomen.

Brachypelma emilia
(White 1856)
Provenance: Mexico
Terrestrial species

B. emilia stays somewhat smaller than *B. boehmei* and usually reaches a body length of 5 to 6 centimeters (2 to 2.4 inches). *B. emilia* is one of the conspicuously marked species. The tibia varies in color from pale beige through yellow to pale orange. The remainder of the leg is black. The cephalothorax is pale beige and has a dark triangle that begins at the eyes and tapers sharply to the rear. The ground color of the abdomen is black with scattered red-brown hairs. Here, too, the terrarium should have an area of 30 x 30 centimeters (12 x 12 inches). *B. emilia* is easy to keep but needs somewhat more moisture than does *B. boehmei*. The tarantulas live in the wild in deep dens under large rocks. As a rule, *B. emilia* mates readily. The cocoon contains several hundred spiderlings that are only a few millimeters long.

Brachypelma smithi
Cambridge 1897
Provenance: Mexico
Terrestrial species

B. smithi probably is the most familiar tarantula of all. Because of its attractive coloration and its peaceful disposition, it is highly prized by many keepers. The ground color of the tarantula is dark brown to black. The patellae of the legs are orange. There are scattered light hairs on the legs. The cephalothorax is dark with a pale beige border and the abdomen is dark with reddish and beige hairs. We should keep the tarantulas in terraria with dimensions of 30 x 30 centimeters (12 x 12 inches). *B. smithi* has a wide distribution in Mexico and occurs in regions with extended dry periods. Therefore, we should not keep it under conditions that are too moist. The species has been bred in captivity many times, which should ensure its survival in our terraria forever. A cocoon contains several hundred spiderlings. *B. smithi* is the only tarantula listed in Appendix II of CITES and therefore is considered an endangered species. The fact is that, according to information from hobbyists who have traveled in Mexico, the population of *B. smithi* has recovered strongly and the tarantulas are encountered very frequently. The species may be traded only with a CITES certificate that gives the provenance of the tarantula. Make sure that the tarantula has such a certificate at the time of purchase.

Brachypelma auratum, female. This tarantula is very hardy. Although it is one of the bombardier spiders, it is a peaceful species.

Brachypelma boehmei, female. This species reaches a body length of up to 7 centimeters (2.8 inches) and is strikingly colored. This is a newly described species that is easy to keep in a fairly arid terrarium climate.

Brachypelma emilia, female.

Brachypelma emilia, male. This tarantula is easy to keep and unproblematic to breed, but it produces many hundreds of spiderlings.

Brachypelma smithi, female.

Brachypelma vagans
Ausserer 1875
Provenance: Colombia,
Costa Rica, Mexico
Terrestrial species
　B. vagans reaches a body
size of approximately 5 to 6
centimeters (2 to 2.4 inches).
The ground color of the
tarantula is black. On the
abdomen there are scattered
red hairs. We should keep B.
vagans in a terrarium with
dimensions of 30 x 30
centimeters (12 x 12 inches).
The species is easy to keep,
though we should keep the
substrate constantly moist.
Mating usually is peaceful,
but we should monitor it. B.
vagans has been bred
frequently in captivity. A
cocoon contains several
hundred spiderlings. As with

B. albopilosa, the species is a
popular tarantula for
beginners because of its
reasonable price and
attractive appearance. It is
not quite as peaceful as B.
albopilosa, though, which is
why we should handle it
somewhat more cautiously.

Ceratogyrus bechuanicus
Purcell 1902
Provenance: South Africa
Terrestrial species
　C. bechuanicus attains a
body length of
approximately 5 centimeters
(2 inches). The species has
a gray ground color and has
dark to black speckling. A
conspicuous feature of all
Ceratogyrus species is the
horn on the cephalothorax
in place of the thoracic

groove that normally is
present in tarantulas. The
individual species can in
part be differentiated on the
basis of the position of the
horn. In C. bechuanicus the
horn curves downward.
Specimens of this species
need a terrarium with
dimensions of 25 x 25
centimeters (10 x 10
inches). The species makes
no special demands with
respect to keeping
requirements, though we
should not keep it under
too-moist conditions. C.
bechuanicus is easy to
breed. We should separate
the tarantulas after mating
and not leave them together
for long in a terrarium. The
tarantulas tend to be
aggressive and do not like to

be picked up. Nonetheless, they are not uninteresting, since they readily spin extensive dens where they stay and into which they retreat when threatened. The species has been bred repeatedly in captivity. A cocoon usually contains approximately 80 to 120 spiderlings. Attempts to crossbreed the species with *C. brachycephalus,* in which the horn curves forward, have produced a surprising result. The spiderlings resulting from this cross have a horn that points vertically upward. Also interestingly, these "hybrids" have been found in the wild in a region where the biotopes of the species *C. bechuanicus* and *C. brachycephalus* adjoin.

Citharacanthus crinirufus
Valerio 1980
Provenance: Costa Rica
Terrestrial species

This species reaches a body length of about 4 to 5 centimeters (1.6 to 2 inches). It is gray in color and has two pale stripes on the legs that curve downward on the patellae. Conspicuous in this species are the metallic blue basal segments of the chelicerae. We should keep the tarantulas in a terrarium with dimensions of at least 25 x 25 centimeters (10 x 10 inches). The species prefers a deep substrate so that it can excavate its den. Furthermore, we should keep the substrate constantly moist. Unfortunately, *C.*

crinirufus is a rare visitor to our terraria because, to my knowledge, it has not yet been bred in captivity. The species also has not been imported frequently, so in the meantime there probably is a shortage of males for breeding. I have no data on breeding. Nonetheless, the species is somewhat aggressive, so we should handle it with care.

Citharischius crawshayi
Pocock 1900
Provenance: East Africa
Terrestrial species

This somewhat unusual species reaches a body length of up to 8 centimeters (3.2 inches), which is a quite impressive size for an African

Brachypelma vagans, female. This tarantula also is easy to keep in the terrarium. It is one of the typical beginner's spiders.

Ceratogyrus hybrid, female. Attempts to cross the species *C. darlingii* with *C. brachycephalus* produced hybrid forms.

Above: Ceratogyrus bechuanicus, female. Below: Ceratogyrus brachycephalus, female.

species. *C. crawshayi* is a light reddish brown color over its whole body and has very short hairs. Females have very robust hind legs that are slightly curved and are used primarily to dig. This species requires special conditions in the terrarium, because the tarantulas excavate very deep dens that in the wild can be up to 2 meters (80 inches deep). It would, of course, be impossible to provide these conditions in a terrarium unless you filled a rain barrel with soil and put the tarantulas in it. Nonetheless, you should try to offer the tarantulas a substrate at least 20 centimeters (8 inches) deep. It is beneficial to use loamy soil as a substrate. You should make sure that the substrate never dries out, since the dens in the wild, because of their depth, constantly are moist. Until a few years ago only the female was known to science. In captivity, however, it turned out that after the first adult molt the males lose their robust hind legs as adults. After some research it was discovered that the males of *C. crawshayi* were known to science after all, but because of their different appearance had been classified in a different genus as a separate species. In the meantime the male had also been described again. Although this species, as all African tarantulas, does not have irritating hairs, it is one of the species that can stridulate the loudest. The tarantulas also are extremely aggressive and are not necessarily recommended to the beginner. The species has

been bred in captivity. The cocoons can contain up to nearly a thousand spiderlings. The spiderlings, however, are very small and grow extremely slowly. It can take up to five years for a juvenile to reach maturity.

Cyriocosmus elegans
(Simon 1889)
Provenance: Venezuela, Tobago
Terrestrial species

C. elegans is one of the dwarf tarantulas (Ischnocolinae) and does justice to its name. It attains a body length of only about 1 centimeter (0.4 inch), but in turn is all the more attractively colored. The cephalothorax is copper-colored with a black triangle, similar to *B. emilia*. The legs are black and silvery on the dorsal side. The abdomen is black with copper-colored stripes on the sides and a heart-shaped blotch on the dorsal side. Because of the small size of the tarantulas, the terrarium need not be particularly large. An area of 20 x 20 centimeters (8 x 8 inches) is quite adequate, but it could also be smaller. The tarantulas like a moist climate and are fond of excavating dens. A planned mating by putting together the two sexes rarely is achieved. We usually must keep the tarantulas together for a fairly long time in the terrarium, which eventually leads to the loss of the male. Nonetheless, the species has been bred in captivity several times. The rearing of the spiderlings presents problems, usually pertaining to the acquisition of food. The spiderlings are so small

that we can offer them only freshly hatched crickets or *Drosophila*. If we can offer the right food, the spiderlings tend to have good appetites and grow to maturity in one and a half to two years.

Ephebopus murinus
(Walckenaer 1837)
Provenance: Brazil, French Guiana
Terrestrial species?

E. murinus reaches a body length of approximately 5 to 6 centimeters (2 to 2.4 inches). It has a dark gray to black ground color, a pale beige cephalothorax, and pale beige stripes on the legs. The fact that the species within the last century was classified in different subfamilies shows that we do not know how the animal should be classified. At present the species is classified in the subfamily Aviculariinae, with the arboreal species. When we keep the tarantulas in the terrarium, however, which should have an area of about 25 x 25 centimeters (10 x 10 inches), it is conspicuous that they not infrequently excavate dens in which they live. Even when we offer them cork tubes or branches they tend to prefer a burrow in the substrate. Concerning the keeping requirements, we should make sure that we keep the substrate constantly moist and spray the terrarium occasionally. The species has been bred in captivity infrequently. During mating, as with *Avicularia*, we can keep the male and female in the same terrarium for several days. The species is not seen often in our terraria. One of the reasons

Citharacanthus crinirufus, female. For this species a fairly deep substrate in the terrarium is preferred so that it can excavate a deep burrow.

Citharischius crawshayi, male. For a long time males of this species were classified in another genus and species. However, it was discovered that the males lose their robust hind legs after the last molt. This was the reason for the incorrect classification.

Cyriocosmus elegans, male. This dwarf tarantula measures only about 1 centimeter (0.4 inch) long.

Ephebopus murinus, female. This species is aggressive and moves very fast.

Grammostola pulchra, female. Because this spider is easy to keep and breed, it is well-suited for the beginner. We must make sure, however, that we keep the substrate in the terrarium moist.

for this is that, if we keep the tarantulas under the correct keeping conditions, they only emerge in late evening. *E. murinus* is a very agile species and also is rather aggressive.

Grammostola pulchra
Mello-Leitao 1921
Provenance: southern Brazil
Terrestrial species

This species reaches a body size of about 6 centimeters (2.4 inches). It is totally black and the hairs have a slight sheen. We should keep this species in a terrarium with an area of about 25 x 25 centimeters (10 x 10 inches). Concerning the keeping conditions, it is important that we keep the substrate constantly moist. The species, as with nearly all *Grammostola* species, has a very peaceful temperament and therefore also is recommended for the beginner. *G. pulchra* is easy to breed. A cocoon usually contains several hundred spiderlings.

Grammostola spatulata
(F. Cambridge 1897)
Provenance: Chile
Terrestrial species

Grammostola spatulata attains a body size of about 5 to 6 centimeters (2 to 2.4 inches). This probably is one of the most frequently imported tarantula species. It is red-brown in color and has a slight pink metallic sheen on the cephalothorax, which is more pronounced in adult males. A terrarium for this species should have an area of 25 x 25 centimeters (10 x 10 inches). The species does not make any special demands in its keeping

requirements, but we should not keep it too moist. As a rule, mating is peaceful. The species is easy to breed. A cocoon usually contains several hundred spiderlings. The species has a peaceful temperament and usually we can pick it up by hand. It is considered to be an excellent spider for the beginner and often is offered by the pet trade. Nonetheless, Chile placed an export ban on animals in mid-1993, which means that in the future this species will seldom be available on the market.

Hysterocrates hercules
Pocock 1899
Provenance: Cameroon
Terrestrial species

This species is among the largest of the African continent. It reaches a body size of 7 to 8 centimeters (2.8 to 3.2 inches) and is uniformly dark brown in color. This species, like *Citharischius crawshayi*, excavates deep burrows and therefore needs a terrarium that can hold a substrate at least 15 centimeters (6 inches) deep. The dimensions of the terrarium should be at least 30 x 30 centimeters (12 x 12 inches). We can mix some sand with the substrate, which should be kept constantly moist. The species has been bred occasionally in captivity. *H. hercules* is aggressive, and we should not pick it up by hand.

Lasiodora parahybana
Mello-Leitao 1917
Provenance: Brazil
Terrestrial species

Lasiodora parahybana is among the largest South

American species and reaches a body length of approximately 9 to 10 centimeters (3.6 to 4 inches) and larger. It is brown in color and has, like *Brachypelma albopilosa*, long, frizzy hairs. Because of its size, a terrarium for this species should have dimensions of at least 40 x 40 centimeters (16 x 16 inches). The species does not make any special demands in the terrarium. It is easy to breed, which, however, subsequently causes some problems. *Lasiodora parahybana* is very productive, and a cocoon can contain up to 1200 spiderlings! This is one reason why this species is rarely bred in captivity. With a single cocoon, the stocks in our terraria are ensured for years. The spiderlings reach maturity in about three years if we feed them a good diet. The species is aggressive and should not be picked up by hand. Males of the species can attain an enormous legspan.

Megaphobema mesomelas
(Cambridge 1892)
Provenance: Costa Rica
Terrestrial species

This beautiful species reaches a body length of approximately 5 centimeters (2 inches). The tarantula has a velvety black ground color and orange-red patellae. The hairs are short. A terrarium for this species should have an area of 30 x 30 centimeters (12 x 12 inches) and be well-ventilated. In the beginning these tarantulas presented serious keeping problems, and many specimens died.

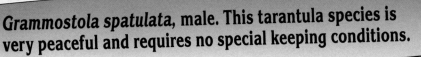

Grammostola spatulata, male. This tarantula species is very peaceful and requires no special keeping conditions.

Grammostola spatulata, female. Females spin a cocoon containing several hundred spiderlings. It is relatively easy to breed.

Hysterocrates hercules, female. As the name indicates, this is a fairly large tarantula, which is why the terrarium should have ample floor space. Because this spider is very aggressive, it should not be picked up by hand, but with forceps.

Lasiodora parahybana, female. This tarantula species is one of the largest tarantulas, and we therefore must keep it in a correspondingly large terrarium.

Pamphobeteus antinous, female. This species is one of the largest tarantulas in the world, for it reaches a length of more than 10 centimeters (4 inches).

Megaphobema mesomelas, female. Only after the detailed study of its biotope was it possible to keep this spider successfully.

Furthermore, until a short time ago virtually no captive breedings were known. A study of the tarantula's biotope in Costa Rica showed that the species occurs in the highlands, where frequent rainfall and constant wind produce a unique climate. The temperatures there seldom rise much above 20°C (60°F). To imitate the climate in the terrarium, as a rule it is sufficient for us to offer the tarantula a constantly moist substrate and to put the terrarium in a not too warm location. Using this method, I have kept this species successfully for several years. Furthermore, the species has been imported again recently and also has been bred in captivity. The tarantulas are slightly aggressive. Breeding in the terrarium is quite difficult and often fails because of the male's timid behavior. This species seems to present a few puzzles to systematists. According to Platnick, the species is in the genus *Euathlus;* according to Smith (personal communication) it is in the genus *Brachypelma;* and according to Schmidt, whom I follow, in the genus *Megaphobema.*

Pamphobeteus antinous
Pocock 1903
Provenance: Bolivia
Terrestrial species

Pamphobeteus antinous is one of the largest tarantula species in the world. It can attain a body length of more than 10 centimeters (4 inches). The tarantulas are uniformly black in color, but the adult males have a metallic blue sheen on the cephalothorax and the dorsal side of the femurs. We should not keep individuals of this species in a terrarium with an area of less than 40 x 40 centimeters (16 x 16 inches). The tarantulas make no special demands concerning keeping requirements. The female that I keep, however, does not take insects and only accepts mice as food. Breeding usually is unproblematic, but offspring, unfortunately, rarely are produced. This is one of the reasons why the species is in such great demand. As a rule, these tarantulas are aggressive.

Pamphobeteus platyomma
Mello-Leitao 1923
Provenance: Brazil
Terrestrial species

This is a species that can attain the quite respectable size of up to 9 centimeters (3.6 inches). These tarantulas are brown to red-brown and have light stripes on the patellae of the legs. The abdomen is dark brown. Adult males have a wine-red metallic sheen on the cephalothorax and the femurs of the legs. A terrarium for this species should have dimensions of 40 x 40 centimeters (16 x 16 inches). These tarantulas make no special demands concerning keeping requirements. These tarantulas mate readily and breeding usually is uncomplicated. The juveniles have an orange-colored abdomen with a black Christmas-tree marking such as is typical of many *Pamphobeteus* species. The spiders lose this coloration at the latest after the juvenile stage. A cocoon of this species usually contains fewer than 100 spiderlings, though they already have a legspan of approximately 2 centimeters (0.8 inches).

Phormictopus cancerides
(Latreille 1806)
Provenance: Brazil, Cuba
Terrestrial species

This species attains a body length of approximately 7 to 8 centimeters (2.8 to 3.2 inches). A few years ago these tarantulas were as common and inexpensive as *Grammostola spatulata* is today, and therefore were very widely distributed. The species is brown in color and has a coppery metallic sheen on the cephalothorax. We should keep *Phormictopus cancerides* in a terrarium with an area of at least 30 x 30 centimeters (12 x 12 inches). Mating usually is unproblematic and breeding is not particularly difficult either. A cocoon can contain up to 150 spiderlings. Unfortunately, the species is somewhat aggressive.

Poecilotheria ornata
Pocock 1899
Provenance: Sri Lanka
Arboreal species

Poecilotheria ornata reaches a body length of about 7 to 8 centimeters (2.8 to 3.2 inches). The species was first offered a few years ago and, because of its attractive appearance, sold for horrendous prices. Each individual of this species has ornamental markings on the dorsal side in shades of light gray to black. The basal segments of the chelicerae are reddish and the undersides of the pedipalps

Pamphobeteus platyomma, female. This tarantula also is one of the largest species and we therefore must keep it in a terrarium with the minimum dimensions of 40 x 40 centimeters (16 x 16 inches).

Pamphobeteus sp., juvenile.

Phormictopus cancerides, female. Because of the reasonable price a few years ago, most tarantula fanciers kept this species.

and the front legs are bright yellow. A terrarium for this species should have an area of 30 x 30 centimeters (12 x 12 inches) and a height of 40 centimeters (16 inches). Because the species lives in tree holes, we can offer it a small birdhouse, which it usually accepts. Some hobbyists keep several females in a large terrarium, each of which lives in its own birdhouse. Because the species lives in the mountainous regions of Sri Lanka, we should keep the species at moderate humidity and not too warm temperatures. For mating it is best to put the male in the female's terrarium for a few days. Everything usually goes well if the female is well-fed. It occasionally happens that the female will eat the cocoon after a few weeks. If breeding is successful, about 80 to 150 spiderlings emerge from the cocoon. The species must be classified as aggressive.

Poecilotheria regalis
Pocock 1899
Provenance: India
Arboreal species

This species attains a body length of approximately 6 to 7 centimeters (2.4 to 2.8 inches). It has ornamental markings that are predominantly light gray in color. The undersides of the front legs are lemon-yellow. We can keep this species under the same conditions as with *Poecilotheria ornata*. The difference is that the temperature and humidity should be higher with this species. The female and male often rest peacefully for weeks at a time in the same

den. A cocoon contains up to 150 spiderlings. Another species that resembles *Poecilotheria regalis* very closely also comes from India. These two species, despite their apparent outward similarity, are easy to tell apart. *Poecilotheria regalis* has a pale beige bar above the epigastric groove on the underside of the otherwise dark abdomen, while the underside of the abdomen of *Poecilotheria fasciata* is uniformly dark.

Psalmopoeus cambridgei
Pocock 1895
Provenance: Trinidad
Arboreal species

Psalmopoeus cambridgei is a species that attains a body length of approximately 6 to 7 centimeters (2.4 to 2.8 inches). It is gray in color and has an orange stripe on the tarsus. A terrarium for this species should have an area of 30 x 30 centimeters (12 x 12 inches) and a height of 40 centimeters (16 inches). This species makes no special demands with respect to keeping requirements, but the conditions should not be too dry. For mating it is best to put the male in the terrarium of the well-fed female for a few days. The species is easy to breed and therefore is widely distributed in the hobby. A cocoon usually holds about 100 spiderlings. If you furnish the terrarium of this species with many roots and branches and leave these furnishings in place for a while, the spider will eventually build a real castle of silk as a nest. These nests can have a diameter of more than 20 centimeters (8

inches). The tarantulas are very fast and somewhat aggressive.

Pseudotheraphosa apophysis
Tinter 1991
Provenance: Venezuela
Terrestrial species

This species reaches a body length of approximately 10 centimeters (4 inches), and therefore is one of the largest tarantula species. This tarantula is uniformly coffee brown in color. Only on the hind part of the abdomen is there a large, dark, round blotch. A terrarium for *Pseudotheraphosa apophysis* should have an area of 40 x 40 centimeters (16 x 16 inches). This tarantula makes no special demands with respect to keeping requirements. This species can be mated without too much trouble, but it has been bred successfully only once. This breeding produced approximately 80 spiderlings. The species was offered initially under the name "*Pamphobeteus exsul*." Later the mistake was discovered and the tarantulas were sold as *Theraphosa leblondi*, which was not correct either. In 1991, I described the species as *Pseudotheraphosa apophysis*. This tarantula is aggressive and is an intense bombardier spider that brushes off its stinging hairs at the slightest disturbance.

Pterinochilus junodi Simon 1904
Provenance: South Africa
Terrestrial species

This medium-sized species attains a body length of about 5 centimeters (2 inches). This tarantula has an attractive coloration. The ground color consists of

Poecilotheria ornata, female.

Poecilotheria ornata, subadult male. This tarantula species is very attractively marked, which affects its price. It lives in tree holes.

Poecilotheria fasciata, female, underside.

Poecilotheria regalis, female. This tarantula also lives in tree holes, which we absolutely must consider when furnishing the terrarium. It usually is easy to breed.

Psalmopoeus cambridgei, female. This tarantula species is widely distributed in the terrarium hobby because it is easy to breed and keep. It builds a large silk nest between objects in the terrarium.

Pseudotheraphosa apophysis, female. At a size of 10 centimeters (4 inches), it is one of the larger tarantulas. It is very difficult to breed.

Stromatopelma calceata, female. Its conspicuous markings give it the popular name "leopard tarantula."

Pterinochilus junodi, female. This is a particularly attractive tarantula species that requires no special keeping conditions.

many shades of brown and gray, and the ginger color of the front legs is particularly striking. We should keep this species in a terrarium with the dimensions 30 x 30 centimeters (12 x 12 inches). It makes no special demands with respect to keeping requirements, but we should not keep it too moist. Mating usually is unproblematic, and approximately 150 spiderlings can emerge from a cocoon. The spiderlings grow quickly when they are well-fed. The species is somewhat aggressive but builds very attractive, large nests of silk, which makes this tarantula particularly attractive.

Stromatopelma calceata
(Fabricius 1793)
Provenance: West Africa
Arboreal species

    Stromatopelma calceata reaches a body length of about 6 centimeters (2.4 inches). It has beige, brown, and black ornamental markings. Because of the markings, it sometimes is called the "leopard tarantula." A terrarium for this species should have an area of 30 x 30 centimeters (12 x 12 inches) and a height of 40 centimeters (16 inches). This species makes no special demands with respect to keeping requirements. For mating, it is best to put the male in the terrarium of the well-fed female for several days. As a rule, the female is not aggressive toward the male.

A cocoon of this species can hold up to 150 spiderlings. The species is very aggressive and fast and therefore must be enjoyed with caution. There are reports of bites from this tarantula, according to which the venom is supposed to be rather strong by tarantula-venom standards. Incidentally, *S. calceata* and *S. griseipes,* which are very similar in appearance, are easy to distinguish if we examine them closely. The femur of the pedipalp is light in color in *S. griseipes* and dark in *S. calceata.*

Theraphosa leblondi
Thorell 1870
Provenance: Brazil, Venezuela, French Guiana
Terrestrial species

    The king of the tarantulas, *Theraphosa leblondi* attains a body length of 12 centimeters (4.8 inches) and a weight of up to 160 grams (5.6 ounces). Some specimens have a legspan of 25 centimeters (10 inches) and more. This species is considered to be the largest spider in the world. It is uniformly coffee brown in color. A terrarium for this species should have an area of at least 40 x 40 centimeters (16 x 16 inches). Concerning the keeping conditions, we should remember that these tarantulas like moisture, therefore we must not keep them too dry. In contrast to the remaining behavior,

mating is extremely peaceful. A cocoon contains up to 100 spiderlings that are already about 20 millimeters (0.8 inches) long when they emerge. *Theraphosa leblondi* is an aggressive tarantula species that is best not touched with the hands. It is one of the bombardier spiders. The irritating hairs of this species seem to be particularly aggressive. The spiders stridulate loudly and intensely when disturbed.

Xenesthis immanis
(Ausserer 1891)
Provenance: Colombia, Venezuela, Panama
Terrestrial species

    This species is quite large and reaches a body size of 8 to 9 centimeters (3.2 to 3.6 inches). The ground color of this tarantula is black. The cephalothorax has a burgundy metallic sheen and the hairs on the abdomen are light brown. We should keep this species in a terrarium with an area of 35 x 35 centimeters (14 x 14 inches). This species makes no special demands with respect to keeping requirements. Unfortunately, it is very difficult to breed. To my knowledge there are no known offspring resulting from a captive breeding. Recently, however, the species has been imported very frequently. *Xenesthis immanis* is an the aggressive tarantula.

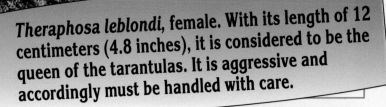

Theraphosa leblondi, female. With its length of 12 centimeters (4.8 inches), it is considered to be the queen of the tarantulas. It is aggressive and accordingly must be handled with care.

Xenesthis immanis, female. This species also grows to a considerable size and also is very aggressive. Accordingly, we must handle it with care.